You're Not Helping...

Ryan Patricks

STORY MERCHANT BOOKS

BEVERLY HILLS

2014

You're Not Helping...

ISBN-10: 0989715493
ISBN-13: 978-0-9897154-9-2

https://twitter.com/Ryan_Patricks

Story Merchant Books
9601 Wilshire Boulevard #1202
Beverly Hills CA 90210

http://www.storymerchant.com/books.html

Editor: Lisa Cerasoli
Interior Design: Lisa Cerasoli and Danielle Canfield
Cover Design: Jillian Bruschera

To my amazing parents:

Dad—you are the funniest person I know.
Mom—I'm so sorry I wrote all of this.

About the Author

For years, Ryan pronounced the word "faux" like "fox," which doesn't sound like that big of a deal until you step into a PETA meeting and tell everyone in the room to relax cause the coat you're wearing is made entirely out of "fox fur." He pulls up too far away from the drive-up ATM and has to get out of his car to take out money. He lives in the hearts of hardworking Americans. Any time a stressed-out waitress prays for the strength to finish another shift or an adorable Puerto Rican baby sees snow for the first time, he is there. In a much more literal sense, he lives in San Francisco, California.

He is twenty-nine years old and has won several international awards for both comedy and lovemaking. He is a personal friend of Jon Stewart and Desmond Tutu. He is also a liar. Some have referred to Ryan as a renaissance man, not because he's skilled in many disciplines, but because he has a 15th century understanding of science and geography. Also, he carries around a sword. He thinks Kanye West is an airline, and Lupe Fiasco is a roller-coaster theme park in Miami. He thinks Zachary Quinto is Spanish for the number twenty-five. He is available for children's parties—not to entertain; he just has a lot of free time[1] and really enjoys cake.

This is Ryan's book—a book where he breaks all the rules. Well, not ALL the rules. The whole pedophile "rule" is definitely not broken, and he doesn't commit tax fraud or anything serious

---

1 Unemployed

like that. When I think about it, he still follows an overwhelming majority of the rules.

Just read the book.

Malcolm Gladwell
(Not *that* Malcolm Gladwell, a different one)

More (than you'll ever want to know) About the Author

Friends often accuse me of being overly self-deprecating and they are 100% right. I'm the worst. What kind of loser is always making fun of himself? I'll tell you who, me. I'm such an ass. Damn it, I'm doing it again!

It's not that I'm depressed or have low self-esteem; I just tend to embody things I dislike. I'm a living decoupage of annoying habits and attributes. For one, I use the word "decoupage." Gross! Also my knees bop, my hands shake, and my feet chafe. Hair grows out of every inch of my body. When I'm in the shower my penis looks like the girl from *The Ring*. If you gave a kindergartner a black crayon and asked her to draw a plate of spaghetti, that is what my asshole looks like—black, rigid, glossy hair growing in every which direction, a tangled web. If I were a redhead, my butthole would look like the hallway towards the bank vault in a heist movie that is guarded with infrared lasers. Catherine Zeta Jones would be dancing her way through it in tights. It's like a smelly cat's cradle. This makes life generally uncomfortable.

Even if you get past the physical stuff, there's a treasure trove of anxious habits and horrible character traits. I was the kid in school that thought if he wrote a sensitive Dave Matthews' lyric on his Jansport, girls would like him. I'm the guy who instead of saying, "I have a girlfriend," would say, "I'm signed to a major labia." That's what I think is funny!

And…it should come as no surprise, that at least three times a day, I hear the phrase, *"You're not helping   "*

"Only pretentious idiots begin their book with a quote from someone."

—Benjamin Franklin

Table of Contents

Introduction

How do you start a book? It's a lot of pressure to be honest with you. The more I think about it, the more I'm kind of freaking out. Oh God, it's like my prom night all over again…I'm alone in my room and on my computer. So, you may be asking, why a book and why now? Well, when I started this book my life was in a vicious downward spiral; like a tornado of anxiety, disappointment and depression. Hold on, do tornados spiral down or up? Actually, I think they spiral up which kind of ruins the metaphor. No one says, "spirals up." That's just stupid. "My life was spiraling up and out of control; I met a beautiful girl, and before I knew it, I got that promotion!" Yep, that does not work. Anyway, the point is I was trying to find a way to channel my depression, and then it hit me—a book! It was like a light bulb went off in my head. I imagine this was how Thomas Edison must have felt when he came up with the actual light bulb. Of course, a light bulb couldn't have gone off in his head because he hadn't invented it yet. I guess an old candle or a dumb oil lamp went off in his head.

I thought writing a book would be a perfect cathartic exercise. For one thing, I like to write. Secondly, you can basically blame any awful behavior on the "creative process," and I had acquired a sufficient amount of "odd behaviors" at this point in my life. So it was a win-win. My first book idea was to chronicle my journey of cooking every single recipe out of the Julia Childs' cookbook, but apparently someone had already done that. Then I thought, how about a book where I find a treasure map on the back of the Declaration of Independence…. But then my publisher pointed out that I hadn't come up with that idea either. I just saw it in a very popular movie. Eventually, I ended up with the pages in front of you now. Trust me, it isn't perfect, but great art rarely is. Look at the Beatles. Eight days a week? Really? I'm sorry, but that just sounds dumb. Get a calendar, Ringo.

I guess I should introduce myself before asking you to read my book. The name is Ryan, but my friends call me, well, like once a month when they need help moving or someone to babysit their dog while they go to Mardi Gras or something. I grew up in the gritty cul-de-sac suburbs of Philadelphia; a true American city. When I think about it, I'm a bit like America myself. For starters, I was conceived in Liberty (Liberty's a dive bar in up-state New York). I also had four fathers! USA, USA, USA!

My childhood was pretty normal. I grew up the middle child of three. As a kid, I was fairly unkempt, always carried around a blanket and had the same gigantic head I have now. Essentially, I was every Peanuts character wrapped into one, without the musical or entrepreneurial skills. I was raised in a loving and traditional Irish Catholic family. If you did not grow up in an Irish Catholic household, it could be hard to explain. The environment is jam-packed with love, fun, and buried resentment. It's a bit like Stockholm Syndrome; that is, if Stockholm Syndrome included first communion parties and a genetic predisposition to rampant alcoholism.

Religion

A Catholic Altered Boy

Religion played an important role in my household growing up. I went to Catholic school my entire academic tenure—from kindergarten to graduate school—but surprisingly; I wouldn't consider myself religious at all. I guess I'd consider myself an agnostic, which is like being an atheist...but for people who are pussies. In fact, I'm pretty sure the word agnostic literally means "wishy-washy" in Latin. Of course, I can't be sure. It's what scholars call, "a dead language."

Like any Catholic kid, I grew up reading and learning about the Bible in elementary school. My favorite story from the Bible is John 7:53-8:11. In this story, a young woman has been caught in the act of adultery, which means cheating on your spouse (I looked it up). I always liked the word "adultery" because it seems to imply that all adults would or should partake in it...simply because they're adults. *Of course I'm being adulterous, I'm thirty years old!* So, the villagers are about to stone this woman for her sin but then Jesus strolls by all chill—presumably on some sort of sweet primitive skateboard he invented—and says, "Let he who is without sin throw the first stone."

This is a favorite story among priests, scholars and general believers who applaud Jesus for making such a compassionate and intelligent point. But what if Jesus just wanted to go first? Maybe he just wanted to show off that carpenter's arm. He probably had a cannon! I bet he pulled that card all the time! "Hold on guys, let he who is without sin, eat the last slice of pizza...oh, yeah, that's me!" It's a flawless strategy. I know I would use it constantly. Then again, I probably shouldn't assume to know what the Son of God did based on what I would do if put in the same situation. I'm pretty sure Jesus wouldn't date the lazy-eyed girl all through grade school just because she had a Sega Genesis.

I also studied the Old Testament in school. The Old Testament is crazy. In it, God is like a girlfriend with borderline personality disorder. Everyone is nailing their sisters and murdering people, too. It's like *True Blood* or Florida. Moses is my least favorite Old Testament character. He always seemed like an annoying hipster with a crazy beard, sandals—always with the sandals, no matter what the weather—and TWO tablets? C'mon, Moses—more like The Burning Bushwick!

Did you know there are thirty different Zechariahs in the Old Testament? Thirty people with the same name like an inverse Tyler Perry movie. And this is back when there were only like 1,000 people on earth. How mad would you be if you named your kid Zechariah, and then one of the fifty other people who existed was like, "Oh, I think I'm going to name my kid Zechariah, too, cause that won't get confusing." It's like sitting down in an empty movie theater and then some other guy walks in and sits in the seat right next to you. It's a clear violation of basic human etiquette. And it's not like anyone had last names. If you said Abraham, everyone knew whom you were talking about because there was only one; it was a great system. The 2nd through 30th Zechariahs ruined that for everyone.

"Hey, have you seen Zechariah?"

"Which one?"

"Umm you know...he's like five foot nothing...wears a robe, Jewish...beard...smells like old bread...lives around here...."

Besides reading lots of Bible stories, growing up in a Catholic household usually meant you were going to spend most of your life confused about sex, which I will make painfully evident throughout this book. Outside of abstinence, my school did not teach or discuss sex. They basically said, "Abstinence is the only 100% effective form of birth control." And then, literally in the next class, taught us about Mary's virgin birth. So it was a tad bit confusing.

Like most of my friends, I got my sex education outside of the classroom but not in the cool way—in the "my parents sat me down and talked about the birds and the bees" way. My parents gave the talk to all three sons at the same time. In retrospect, my older brother was the only one who was mature enough to understand it. Nonetheless, my parents gathered us into the family room. They sat behind us on an old weathered couch while we congregated, as we always did, Indian-style on the floor as close to the TV as possible. Not surprisingly, our parents didn't mind our sitting as far away from them as we could this particular night.

My parents then put on an informational video that explained all the ins and outs (elbow poke) of sex. The show itself was somewhat of a blur. The only part I can remember now is the segment on erections. As they explained that the male penis can, in fact, enlarge and get hard; I jumped up proud as a peacock and yelled, "That happens to me when I think about girls with guns!"

My parents erupted into laughter. It would mark the first, but definitely not the last time people would openly laugh at my erection. At the time, I wasn't sure if it was the idea of girls or the idea of guns that gave me an erection. But either way, when *Laura Croft Tomb Raider* came on TV this Thanksgiving, my mom turned red and quickly changed the channel. When I think about this dick-declaration now, I feel really strange and uncomfortable. It's a hard emotion to describe. It's the same feeling I get when I see a grown adult riding in the backseat of a car. It's a feeling that would accompany me through most of my life.

Some say that you're never too young to learn about sex education, but I disagree. Learning adult things before you're "adult enough" to understand them can be dangerous. When I first started learning about girls and the female anatomy, they showed me this diagram to explain the female reproductive system.

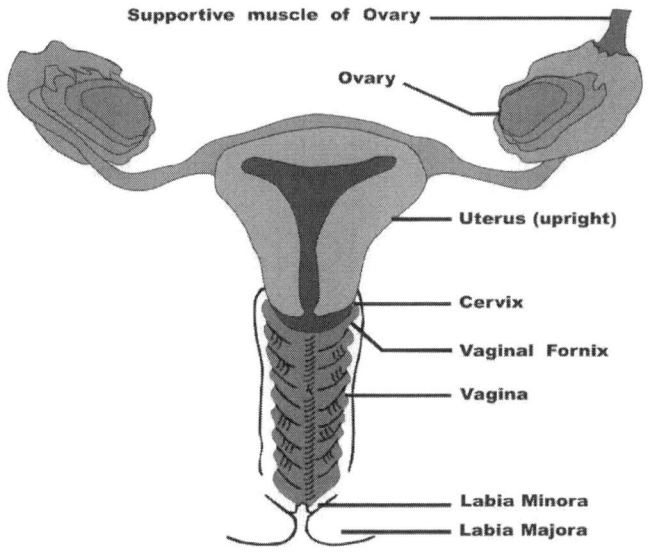

Being too young to wrap my head around this diagram, I thought that whole "situation" was outside the body as an appendage...and to be honest it scared the hell out of me. Look at that thing. It's horrifying! It's like a bloody bear's face with a screwdriver walrus tusk. I wish I could say that this is the reason I was a virgin until I was nineteen[2], but I think my hostage-like comfort level in social situations deserves most of the credit for that feat.

Sebastian

Shortly after the sex talk, I received the Sacrament of Confirmation. You typically receive this sacrament in or around the 8th grade, and it's supposed to bless you with the gift of the Holy Spirit. The Holy Spirit is kind of like the ghost version of God; he's a little bit more mysterious and cooler than God the Father and Jesus. Comic books and fantasy novels use this character device all the time. In the *X-Men*, Jean Grey dies only to be reborn as the more powerful Phoenix. In *Lord of the Rings*, Gandalf falls down a bottomless pit but returns to the world as the super-powered Gandalf the White. It's a common storyline and mythology in the comic book community—which technically is the only community more frightened by the vagina than the religious community.

In the Sacrament of Confirmation, you select a confirmation name, which is a name you pick to add to your actual name. Unfortunately, you can't pick good names like Sting or Oprah; it

---

2 Twenty-three

has to be a saint's name (and despite my mom's constant declarations, Oprah is not a saint). My confirmation name is Sebastian, which I hate. Sebastian is a terrible name. After a few years I found out about St. Blaze. Blaze?! Are you kidding me?! I could have chosen Blaze?! This bothered me at two separate and equally embarrassing phases of my life: when I got really into rollerblading, and when I got really into Phish.

So why did I pick Sebastian? Well, like most of my religious commitments, it was the result of deep-seeded Catholic guilt. I was a bit of an existential 8th grader and wanted to pick a name that had meaning—like a spring break co-ed who got a tattoo of a Chinese symbol that she thought meant "strength," but really meant "handicapped parking."

Now, despite having the athletic prowess of a drunken Queen Elizabeth on rollerblades, I prided myself as an athlete in my younger days. In reality, the only thing I truly excelled at was eating the oranges my mom would bring for halftime. Oh, and striking out on attempted bunts as the only little leaguer on the team who required an adult-sized batting helmet for his massive head. I looked up the patron saint of athletes in my new book. Low and behold it was Sebastian. Disappointed, I immediately dismissed the idea of picking such a nerdy name. I already had enough trouble making friends as the only kid at the cafeteria table without pizza Lunchables or a cool Starter jacket. Then my mom unleashed some good old-fashioned Catholic guilt on me about choosing a name for the right reasons. So, despite searching for a manly name, I was stuck with the name of the cartoon singing crab in a popular Disney movie. I was humiliated.

Over the coming weeks, I learned about Sebastian. To prepare for the sacrament, we had to write a full report on our patron saint. Turned out Sebastian was not an athlete at all. Sebastian was best known for being shot up with a quiver of arrows for being Christian and denouncing the king. That was hardly a sport. In fact, it's almost the opposite of archery. I could maybe understand it if it were on purpose like he was some sort of "arrow goalie" or something. But I looked into it, and that was definitely not the case. Sebastian was left for dead, but miraculously ended up surviving the arrow attack. Later, once he healed up, he went back to the king and denounced him in person. This time, the king had him beaten to death with clubs and bats. Personally, I think Sebastian may have been the patron saint of "not learning his lesson the first time." That would at least explain why I'm a shitty athlete and why I keep watching *Fast and Furious* movies. Instead, Sebastian is the patron saint of athletes and archers. So, to recap: he never played a sport, was shot with a ton of arrows and then beaten to death with clubs and bats, and the Church made him the patron saint of athletes and archers! Essentially, we made him the patron saint of people who brandish clubs, bats or bows. That means someone trying to shoot something with an arrow or hit something with a bat, may actually pray to Sebastian for help. Why would we do that to him? If I were Sebastian, I would never want to see an arrow, archer or bat again. That's like making JFK the patron saint of sharpshooters, or Elvis the patron saint of bacon cheeseburgers.

Catholic Guilt

One of my earliest memories is the first time I stole something, besides Libby Gibson's heart in second grade. High five! I was probably eleven years old, and I was at the supermarket with my mom. As we made our way through the bright, linoleum aisles—picking up that week's supply of peanut butter, bread and pretzel rods that would comprise my school lunch every day from 1st to 9th grade—I came across several bins of Hershey Chocolate Miniatures. One miniature caught my eye, "Special Dark." Instantly my heart fluttered. I had never heard of special dark chocolate before. I thought; chocolate is already special, so this must be amazing! How can you make chocolate more special? My world was immediately flipped upside down; black was white, white was black...time stood still. Keep in mind, I was too young to know how to masturbate or buy Cinnabons at this point, so chocolate was a kind of demigod in my life. Knowing my mom would never let me have chocolate that late in the day, or ever, I discreetly reached into the bin, snagged one, and tucked it safely away in my neon Umbro windbreaker pocket. (Yes, I had a neon Umbro windbreaker. Calm down, ladies'.)

After a seemingly never-ending car ride, we arrived home. I locked myself in my room and pulled out the chocolate, like Gollum would the ring. As I cradled it like a dumpster baby brought into a rectory, a massive wave of guilt washed over me. I had stolen something and stealing was wrong. I momentarily fought off the guilt and bit the miniature in half. What I tasted was the worst taste I could've ever imagined. It was as if all my taste buds took a shit in my mouth at the same time. It was so bitter! I freaked out. I figured God must have robbed the sweetness from the candy as a punishment for stealing. It was the only thing that made sense. Clearly, Hershey would not make a bitter, horrible chocolate bar and then call it "special." That's like naming a sporting event where no one is any good "The Special Olympics." Wait. Bad example. Anyway, I spent the next few weeks praying more and being extra nice to my family and friends.

No matter how much I try to shake them, my Irish Catholic roots are deep, like hipster V-neck deep. I've tried to be more religious as an adult. A few months ago I decided to read the Bible from start to finish. I made my way through two thirds of it and was reading it on the subway in Philadelphia when this crazy homeless guy came up to me and yelled "Jesus died for your sins!" right in my face. I was totally taken aback by his rudeness. Who just blurts out something like that? It was a total spoiler alert! He could clearly see that I hadn't finished the book yet. "Way to ruin it for everyone!" I yelled back and added, "Snape killed Dumbledore!" but he just looked confused...and dirty, really, really dirty.

Since then, I have mainly ended my long-dying relationship with religion. I find most religious people to completely infringe on everyone else's right to self-determination. It's not enough to have your own belief system; everyone else has to have your belief system, too. The only other people who do that are people who like avocados. I never understood that logic. It became too clear how religion made some people crazy, especially since radical Islam grabbed the American public's attention after 9/11. Religious zealots had ruined lives, communities, and even many of the small pleasures we took for granted.

Little things like the word "radical." Radical used to be an awesome thing to be. It meant you skateboarded or played electric guitar. A radical party meant an 80's style kegger followed by a make-out session with a girl who has a tongue ring. Now it means a political group that wants to cut your head off. Radical used to mean wakeboarding or snowboarding, and now it means water boarding. We have religion to thank for that.

Me Today

An average day for me is a lot like that David Bowie song "Space Oddity." This isn't because I am embarking on a dangerous and significant adventure or because I have a well-respected and unique job, but because it begins with someone telling me to take my pills and put my helmet on. I am twenty-nine years old, but, unfortunately, I still think like a twelve-year-old. I can't walk through an Ikea without fantasizing about having a laser tag game in there. I can barely function in the adult world. The other week I made a friend miss a flight because I knowingly drove him to the arriving gates. I did this because I thought, "Well, I'm *arriving* at the airport in my car...I'm not leaving it." That's how dumb I really am. I also sleep constantly; the doctors aren't sure if I have Narcolepsy or just "no general direction in life." I feel like I'm at a point in my life that is a limbo between the responsibilities of adulthood and the reckless abandon of youth—a literal "No Man's Land," if you will. I'm desperately clinging to youth as long as I can. It's like Raiders of the Lost Ark; I'm Indiana Jones and the rolling boulder behind me is adulthood. I'm running from the boulder towards "short round" who represents mischief and youth—with his wide eyes and adorable Yankee's cap—but deep down I know those ten-year-old Asian limbs are short, and there is no way we are outrunning that bolder for long. I know that sooner or later I will have to grow up. Sooner or later I will see the day where I am enough of an adult to combine scenes from Raiders of the Lost Ark with characters from Temple of Doom in a terrible metaphor and not feel conflicted about it, but unfortunately...that day is not today.

It's not that I'm scared of being old or unwilling to embrace my ultimate inescapable demise in some existential sense. To be honest, I'm scared of being middle-aged. Being old actually sounds great to me: you get unlimited prescription pills, cell phones with only three buttons and a free pass for being rude to people. Also, I will finally be able to go out in public with a blanket over my lap without anyone thinking something "creepy" is going on. It sounds magical! It's the thirty years before old age that frightens me most. PTA meetings, 401Ks, cleaning out gutters while avoiding eye contact with your next-door neighbor, taxes, discovering new pains, going to the gym to maintain a train wreck of a physique—these are the things my nightmares are made of. I am a twenty-nine-year-old man who recently nicknamed his own balls, "The Wrinklevoss Twins." I have no place in the world of bills, insurance policies and general responsibility.

I'm basically a child masquerading as an adult. I have been accused of being a hipster but to be fair, my blue-collar GED friends who have made this claim consider anyone who flosses or has seen a non-Fast and Furious movie, a hipster. Hipster-ness is a continuum—a skinny jeans spectrum. I like Wes Anderson but I've never grown an ironic mustache, so I'm probably towards the middle. I've never fully understood the hipster movement. It seems like a sad attempt to distinguish oneself with some obscure ironic joke that outsiders just don't know about. Like most "great" Caucasian cultural movements, hipster-ness seems to be more about exclusion than anything else. Unfortunately, a lot of art and music I enjoy are used as the means to that exclusion. So, since I like hoppy beers and street art, I am a hipster? And for a group that prides itself on being unique, most of the hipster movement seems like it was borrowed from rural farmers anyway. Think about it. It started with fear of the government. Then it was flannels, drinking out of mason jars and eating organic. Pitchfork Magazine? -Sounds like farmers to me. I'm very confident that the next "hip" thing is coming right out of the farming culture, or as I call it, "agri-culture." (See what I did there?) That is why I have recently started growing corn and also being super racist to people.

I'm an early adopter I guess.... (You probably wouldn't get it.)

Excerpts from Diary #1

November 11, 2013

Dear Diary,

Today in my psychology class my friend mispronounced Schadenfreude and then someone called him an idiot in front of the whole class. It made me feel really happy.

July 4, 2013

Dear Diary,

Rented that movie Hancock for the 4th of July, and I have to say, Will Smith's portrayal of John Hancock didn't seem very historically accurate. I mean he got some things right, sure, but overall it felt a little embellished. And you don't need to embellish America. It's already awesome. USA! These colors do not run...or even mildly speed walk. That's probably why we lead the world in obesity.

July 25, 2011

Dear Diary,

The NFL lockout is over. Thank God! The only alternative place to watch repressed gay men working on conversions every Sunday would be Church.

December 12, 2011

Dear Diary,

My grandma is sooo lame. She's been planking on the kitchen floor for like three hours. Planking is like so six months ago....

Things I Love

Google

There are lots of things I love. Dogs in sunglasses for one thing. I also love movies about guys who dress up like girls to lead a soccer team to a championship, and any show about a "rogue agent." But one thing I love almost more than anything is technology. I could write an entire book about the joy of Google. It may be the single most influential company/invention of my generation. I love Google. I can get directions to the planetarium while simultaneously looking up what a planetarium is and how to pronounce it. It is great. If there is one downside to Google, it's that this single invention has ruined the art of bullshitting forever.

There was a time before Google when you could vehemently defend your own bullshit and even if someone called you out; it was at best a "he said, she said" argument. You could be at the museum (or planetarium I think) and say, "Oh, I love Van Gogh paintings. Did you know he sketched *Starry Night* in an absinthe bar? That's why it's all distorted." Then one of your friends might say, "I heard he painted it from an asylum in France." At this point, you would know the lie you just made up to look smart is in question amongst the group, and your credibility would be on the line. This meant you would have to ramp up the bullshit by trying to sound even more knowledgeable and confident: "Naw, man, you're confusing it with *The Potato Eaters. Starry Night* was way before he was taken away. He was committed after his brother Theo died which was way later." Now you have probably reclaimed your status as *smart guy* amongst your friends through complete bullshitting.

Before Google, if your friend really wanted to prove you wrong, he would have to spend his Sunday in a library and get on microfiche or something stupid like that and make a nerdy little book report. Then he would have to find you and your friends a week later and be like, "Hey guys, remember that argument we got in a week ago? Well, it turns out Ryan was wrong!" Then everyone would look at each other like this guy is nuts for investing all this time into it. Again, you remain victorious as you gently say, "Oh, I guess you were right, buddy," while glancing at your friends with a "this guy's a psycho" look.

Unfortunately, Google has single-handedly destroyed this ability. No more bullshitting your way through a French film, no more rants at the planetarium, no more tricking girls to hang out with you at the bar by claiming you were in that movie *The Sandlot* or invented those shoes with wheels in the heel. The days of bullshitting are over. It's true, just look it up on Google.

Twitter

I love Twitter. Twitter is like a drunken sorority girl: half of what she says is slurred, she loves Ashton Kutcher and commonly misses periods. The only difference is that Twitter is totally down to hang out with me. Sometimes I wonder how Twitter got so popular. It's essentially an extremely limited blogging service with a dashboard. I think the popularity of Twitter is a testament to how often people want to hear other people talk on the Internet. Cause, let's be honest; no one cares about your cat blog. Blogs are like kids or art, when it's your own you think it's amazing, but honestly, no one else cares. Twitter cashed in on that idea by turning the six-page blog post into 140 characters, which is just short enough for people to tolerate reading. I think 141 characters must be the tipping point (Malcolm Gladwell reference, business stuff) right before someone says, "Oh, shut the fuck up about your breakfast, Ryan, no one cares!"

At first, I had trouble fully embracing Twitter. As a result, most of my followers were porn sites or bots, which was annoying. If you would've told me ten years ago that one day I would be slightly annoyed that robots and porn stars were "following me," I would've said you were lying. Ecstatic? Maybe. Terrified? Probably. But definitely not "slightly annoyed." If porn stars and robots were following you in 1993, it meant something terrifying and/or awesome was going to happen to you. These days I unabashedly love Twitter. Honestly, what's not to love? It's like cocaine: it's addictive; all the celebrities are on it, and you can do it off your iPhone in a bathroom stall at work.

Comic Books

I love comic books. I read tons of comic books growing up. I loved *Marvel, DC*...everything. That is everything except *Captain America. Captain America* is a story about a guy who is injected with a serum that gives him crazy muscles and then he becomes an American icon and spends his entire career combating a German Nazi stereotype. The whole thing reminded me too much of Arnold Schwarzenegger; I couldn't get into it. Other than that, I was obsessed with the superhero world. It was a place where anything could happen. Every character had the potential to be a hero and, of course, all the girls had huge awesome racks. I think I liked the idea of being special. Since I was a small child, I always wanted to be special, like "it rains when I'm sad" special.

Comic books allowed me to deeply indulge the fantasy that I had some secret power just waiting to be unleashed—a potential that was limitless.

Even when lost in the make believe world of comics, I found myself questioning certain things. For example, Gotham and Metropolis were part of America. In these comics, they would mention American cities and other real-life places, so it was clear that Gotham and Metropolis existed in some version of our world. Yet for some reason, criminals continually tried to rob banks that were like two blocks away from Superman's or Batman's apartment. I was probably only ten, but I remembered thinking: *Why would anyone choose Metropolis to commit a crime? They do know a fucking superhero lives there, right? Do they think they're going to be the first criminal to successfully rob Metropolis Bank...EVER?!* I mean; the criminals must have known about Superman, right? I don't watch a lot of news, but I think if there was a flying man who was constantly saving the world—specifically one city—I probably would have heard about him. I'm just saying Detroit does not have any superheroes. I would think it'd be well worth the gas money.

Sometimes I wonder about the more personal aspects of my favorite superheroes' lives—the stuff the comics never had the time to get into. What is Batman's favorite pizza topping? Is Spiderman a democrat? Does Aquaman have a penis inferiority complex (shrinkage)? Here are some thoughts on what the potential musical tastes of my favorite superheroes were and why:

Batman is a fan of Emo:

- Super rich white kid with emotional issues after his parents are murdered
- Loves technology
- Hangs out in a dark cave on his computer
- Never gets the girl

Spiderman must listen to Rap:

- He lives in Queens with his Auntie
- Someone carjacked and shot his uncle on the block
- His main interest is Mary Jane
- Constantly profiled by the police

Superman is an Indie Rock guy:

- Works as a journalist
- Wears hipster glasses and tight graphic tees
- Is against conglomerates like LexCorp

Professor X is into Techno:

- Loves cutting edge technology
- Very cerebral
- Uses few words
- Is always "rolling"

Thor is all about Dub-step:

- Thor is a tool

Movies

There are few things I love more than going to the local theater for a moving picture show. I grew up on movies. A lot of therapists and cultural historians say movies influence how we develop, and ultimately forge the people we become...but I think that's pure bull-spit. I grew up constantly watching *Winnie the Pooh,* and it had no effect on me whatsoever! I mean, I'm a slightly pudgy, effeminate man who rarely wears pants and can't spell the word "huney" correctly; but other than that, no harm done! Movies are still a huge part of my life. I practically live at the theater. As we speak, I am in the theater watching a movie entitled *Gnomeo and Juliet.* And I have to tell you, I smell Oscar! Unfortunately, Oscar is the name of the small Filipino boy next to me covered in juice.

I personally think this generation has seen a golden age in television and a golden-shower age in films. We are defined by *Breaking Bad* but also *White Chicks*; *Arrested Development*...and also *Hitch*. We are the age of the *Simpsons* and, unfortunately, *Simpsons the Movie.*

"Rufio, Rufio, Rufio!"
One of the first movies I can remember really enjoying was *Hook*; I used to play *Hook* all the time and memorized half the movie. *Hook* is essentially a continuation of the Peter Pan story. It's got it all—lost boys, flying, swords and scary pirates. When you think

about it, pirates are the only group that was really into rape who we still culturally celebrate, besides professional athletes, of course. To this day I still insert *Hook* jargon into my everyday life, and you should too. Here is how to do it:

1. When someone's cell phone goes off in the movie theater yell, "Bad form, Peter!" in your best Captain Hook voice. Everyone will laugh (on the inside).

2. When your girlfriend begs you to propose already, get on your knees and put a thimble on her finger.

3. When you take your five-year-old cousin along with you to Camden to buy drugs and he says, "I just want to go home," say, "But Jack, you are home," and then kick him out of the car and drive off. Leave him there for a few minutes. Sure, he'll be pissed for a while but once he gets older he'll probably think that was hysterical.

4. If you're ever in a clock store, just start breaking everything and yell, "This is for not letting me blow bubbles in my chocolate milk!" If the storeowner starts screaming at you, then you can say, "Somebody needs a mommy very badly," in a super cute voice.

Twilight

One of the strangest fads of this generation has been the explosion of vampire culture. Now, I'm not saying I like *Twilight*, but I do think the fascination with vampires is interesting. Vampire-loving tweens flocked like never before to go to the theaters and see *Twilight*—which is the flagship of the vampire craze. I never got the appeal of *Twilight*, personally. I always thought Robert Pattinson looked like a real life Derek Zoolander. His face is in constant blue steal! Also, taken at face value, the plot is actually pretty creepy. The main male character, Edward, is a vampire, and he is 109 years old but pretends to be in high school. He starts dating Bella, who is seventeen. This means Edward is really just an old, pale, pasty, pedophile pretending to be in high school to pick up minors. This guy shouldn't be considered sexy; he should be prohibited from living within 500 feet of a daycare center.

What I did like about the movie was Bella's father. Now granted, I did not watch the whole thing so maybe he turns into a dragon or something stupid like that later in the movie.... But from what I saw, he was a stand-up guy with a respectable moustache and a pick-up truck. He probably loves over-processed breakfast meat and Billy Joel. He's the embodiment of Americana—the last of a dying breed. I hope one day to be a similar father; a perfect blend of masculinity and compassion. Sure, I may own a hunting rifle, but that doesn't mean I can't sit down with my daughter and have an honest conversation about the dangers of dating horny werewolves.

Teen Movies

I have a special place in my heart for movies about kids going to high school. You can always tell it's one of those movies cause the opening scene is a first-person point of view weaving through a school. Apparently, Hollywood thinks that, at every high school, there are kids doing perfect kick flips and cool Asian kids break dancing between classes. This is NOT the case, Hollywood. Believe me, I spend a lot of time just sitting in a local high school's parking lot...and none of that ever happens. (I have hours of videotapes to prove it too.)

(Note to the editor: Lisa, can you delete the part about sitting in a high school parking lot filming kids; I probably shouldn't have shared that. It could probably get me in some trouble. Thanks!)

The Little Mermaid

The Little Mermaid is also a childhood favorite. My favorite *The Little Mermaid* scene is when Arial combs her hair with a fork on her first date with the prince. The prince totally plays it off like, "Oh, you are just adorably quirky, like a Zooey Deschanel." But in his head you know he was like: *Oh, God, she's retarded. She literally just called the fork a dingle hopper, then she tried to comb her hair with it. Oh, God, her Grandmother/guardian is probably searching for her at the YMCA right now. Why does this always happen to me? I finally get a hot redhead back to my place, and she has a serious mental disability. Damn it! Oh, God, she thinks the pipe is a whistle! SHE THINKS THE PIPE IS A WHISTLE! Just laugh it off, Eric. She's fine. She's fine, just kidding around. Yeah, that's all. She's just trying to be funny;*

you know, funny-haha. Nothing illegal going on here…. Fuck. Who am I kidding?! This is bad…this is real bad. Would it be wrong of me, if I still, ya know, went for it? I mean; c'mon, look at her! Know what? I'm going for it, I don't care…I don't even care. I'm getting married soon; this is going be my last chance. She's okay. She's totally joking around. Yup….

This is me guessing what happens in movies I've never seen:

- *How Stella Got Her Groove Back*: Tinder?
- *Up*: An old pedophile steals kid in balloon house?
- *Gran Torino*: Racist grandpa gets new neighbors…isn't happy.
- *The Village*: Joaquin Phoenix whispers a lot, annoys people.
- *Snatch*: Cool, ironic nicknames in accents I don't understand.
- *My Girl*: Nerdy kid dies from a peanut allergy or something lame. Everyone cries.
- *The Hunger Games*: My girlfriend sees how late she can make us for our dinner reservations.

This is me renaming movies because sometimes the titles just aren't very clear:

- *The King's Speech: Tale of The Mush-Mouth King*
- *Black Swan: The Scariest Boner Ever*
- *Social Network: Revenge of the Nerds 5*
- *I Am Legend*: (About a desolate place filled with guns, pale disgusting creatures and one Black guy): *Sioux Falls, South Dakota.*

Music

I am a big fan of music. I even write "Music" on my resume in the Interests section right next to Dream Journaling and Freestyle Walking. This way I can differentiate myself from other candidates. That is just basic Business 101, but I'll save awesome tips like that for my next book: *An Advanced Guide to Cloud Watching and Business Stuff*. I am also a musician myself. I play in a Crazytown cover band. But to be honest, it's not doing too hot. The rest of the guys in Insane City (including me) may be calling it quits. But my love for music will always remain. I enjoy most types of music, but I particularly like old soul and blues stuff. Sometimes I get upset that I never got to see my hero, Ray Charles, in concert. Sometimes I get upset that Ray Charles never got to see himself in concert...or anywhere really. Here are some of my thoughts on music:

Brand New: If I were in the band Brand New, I would name my first album *Their Recent Album*. This would allow pretentious kids to say, "I like old Brand New music like their old album: *Their Recent Album*." I think that would get other people confused and annoyed enough to resort to violence.

Lady Gaga: I have a real bone to pick with Lady Gaga. Like eight years ago I bought this sweet cat and named it Lady Gaga and then like a year later some eccentric chick that looks like a young

Mr. Burns in a blonde wig comes on to the scene and totally ruins it for me. I mean, WTF you guys! Now I have to put my cat down cause some transsexual super villain from the future got famous?! It's ridiculous! I mean, this girl looks like she dresses using a mad lib:

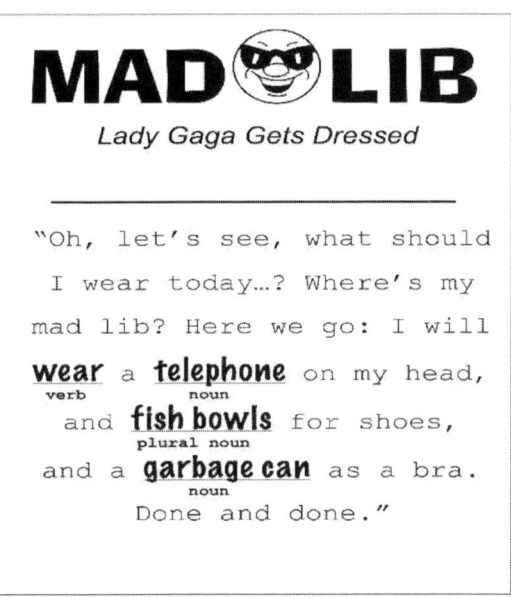

Zeppelin: Ever since *Lord of the Rings* came out, some of my favorite Zeppelin songs just seem nerdy. Take this verse from their 1969 smash, "Ramble On:"

"T'was in the darkest depths of Mordor,

I met a girl so fair,

But Gollum and the evil one crept up

And slipped away with her."

When I used to listen to Zeppelin, I would imagine destroyed hotel rooms, groupie orgies and midgets covered in cocaine juggling bags of heroin. Now I imagine four guys hanging around a Dungeons and Dragons board game comparing retainers.

Queen: I literally just learned that in Queen's "Bohemian Rhapsody" they are saying, *"Will you let him go? Bismillah!"* I always thought they were saying, "Ms. Miller." You know, I thought it was strange that this random spinster, Ms. Miller, was the lady who could decide whether or not this kid went to jail. He murdered someone for Christ's sake, and it's up to some substitute math teacher if he gets off the hook? So, yeah, Bismillah makes more sense.

Ironically Accurate Album Titles:
1. Britney Spears: *Blackout*
2. Elliott Smith: *A Brief History*
3. Michael Jackson: *Keep it in the Closet*
4. R Kelly: *That's that shit!*
5. Adam Sandler: *What the Hell Happened to Me*
6. Heidi Montag: *No More*

Books

I love books. Having the time to sit down with a good book is an amazing feeling. It's like finding money in an old pair of

Levis...and the guy wearing them on the subway doesn't even wake up when you fish it out of his pocket. To be fair, I wasn't much of a reader outside of my school's mandated summer reading assignments. I remember thinking Anne Frank's diary was surprisingly different from Lisa Frank's diary. I still wonder if they were sisters or something. But one of those girls was pretty outgoing, and the other really kept to herself, so I kind of doubt it. I do think if Anne Frank had written her diary in a Lisa Frank diary, it would have been way less depressing. I know it's nearly impossible to brighten up persecution, Nazis and genocide...but then again, glitter and rainbows can go a long way. Did you know that glitter has been scientifically proven to repel sadness? It's true. That's why we put it on strippers. In all honesty, *The Diary of Anne Frank* was an amazing and inspiring work. I was actually lucky enough to visit the Anne Frank House while in Amsterdam in my early twenties. As a tourist, there were maps and pamphlets with directions to the Anne Frank House everywhere you go. So I'm kind of surprised it took the Germans so long to find it. They should have just asked a tour guide or something. But you know us men—*never willing to ask for directions....*

My love affair with the written word has led me to the local library many a night. I'll grab a coffee, find a spot where everyone can see me being smart, then pretend to be invested in a book while looking for cute girls to notice how sophisticated I am—you know...reading! Sometimes when I'm feeling a bit puckish (look

it up), I go to the mystery section and hide a bloody glove between shelves or write a cryptic name in a matchbook and place
it next to a hangman's noose. Similarly, sometimes I'll even put
an unassembled bird feeder in the Hobbies & Trades section. I
like to think I'm turning someone's fantasy into a reality, but in
truth I'm probably just pissing off a janitor.

Excerpts from Diary #2

December 22, 2011

Dear Diary,

My girlfriend stole my solitaire cards today...well, two can play that game! Actually, it's more of a one person game, but I mean I'm going to steal something of hers.

January 10, 2012

Dear Diary,

I wonder if Jackson Pollock peed on the seat a lot...?

March 12, 2012

Dear Diary,

For her birthday, I took my Grandma to the Antiques Road-show. Turns out she's only worth like 52 bucks. Very disappointing.

August 16, 2012

Dear Diary,

I realized today that I have two big fears in life. The first is dying alone. The second is having a Frisbee land next to me in the park and hear someone yelling, "Hey, little help?"

August 17, 2012

Dear Diary,

I got called into the Philadelphia Police Department for reported reckless driving this morning, which over the phone sounds a lot like wreck-less driving. So, I walked in pretty enthusiastic. I was expecting a medal, not a $500 fine.

Stuff I Hate

Baby Talkers

I hate baby talkers. Now, I want to be very clear, I'm not talking about the *Look Who's Talking* trilogy. Talking babies are hilarious. C'mon, Kirstie Alley as a chubby, slobbering baby who shits her pants every time she doesn't get her way?! It works for her in real life too! Not to mention the cover has a baby wearing neon sunglasses on it. SUNGLASSES! It's like, how does this *baby* have such an *outrageous* fashion sense? It's only a baby! Now that is comedy. I think I made my point. Do yourself a favor and rent them tonight. They won't let you down.

Now what I hate are parents who use baby talk when talking to their babies. First of all, parents stink. Just the other day this mom gave me the dirtiest look cause I *pretended* to put my electronic cigarette out on her baby's forehead. It's called comedy, lady. Parents who use baby talk are especially the worst. These are the parents who will hand the baby juice while saying, "You want your juicy wuicy wuicy?" Your kid does not calls it "juicy wuicy" cause he thinks it's cute. He calls it that because he doesn't understand how words work yet. His mash potato brain is trying its best...but it's a baby, and they suck at almost everything. You have no excuse as a parent to do that. Your stupid baby is going to think juicy wuicy is the right way to say "juice" and eventually and you'll have to home school him and get him speech therapy and the other kids will throw batteries at him and call him "Cwying Wyan Patwicks" or something like that. So don't do that.

Specials

Despite adhering to a strict diet of Del Taco and Tums, I will sometimes join friends and family for a dining experience, and while I already abhor these times, I particularly dread the moment when the waiter says, "Would you like to hear our specials?"

It's the worst! You can't say "no thanks." It's impossible! Try saying, "no" the next time a waiter asks you if you want to hear the specials and see the looks you get from the table.

"Ryan! We have to hear them! They are special!"

Hearing the specials is like when you have to look at Peggy's new baby from accounts receivable. You have to pretend that Garbage Pail Kid is a Picasso, but all you're thinking about is whether or not there will be bagels in the break room and if you can postpone the murder/suicide thoughts long enough to smile effectively while walking to the water cooler.

Now the waiter plunges into a rehearsed thirty-minute diatribe about how the carrot soup—that no one wants—is prepared. Most of the time the waiter will look up and to the left just to remember the whole thing. It's like speech day in English class all over again except you aren't high. While he's sounding off like an NPR reporter, all the people at your table are oohing and aahing at every special like it's a goddamn *Chris Angel Mindfreak* episode, and they're uttering practically in sync "that sounds good, that sound good." It's as if not complimenting the specials would somehow offend the waiter, like he personally spent all night creating the dishes himself.

Then after all of that, after all the awkward eye contact, after all that time and fake excited looks, no one ever gets the specials! That's because they suck, and you were too busy pretending to be interested to even hear them.

People Who Eat in Grocery Stores

People who eat in grocery stores drive me crazy, like "Paul at the end of Hey Jude" crazy. What is the matter with these people? It's not a restaurant. Can you not go twenty minutes without cramming food in your face? Honestly, I've seen more restraint from raccoons in a dumpster. The rest of us shoppers really love the smell of Cheetos in the air and double chocolate frosting smeared on the carts. Every time I see someone bring a handful of crumb-filled wrappers to a cashier to ring up, I just want to throw an apple at their Hulk-sized heads, but I don't. Because I have an ounce of impulse control.

Note: Above does not apply to the free cookies given away at the bakery, especially if you are a member of the Cookie Club. And there is nothing on the official Cookie Club website that says you have to be younger than eleven years old to be a member. So, you can tell Mr. Garner to go ahead and call security again. I have a printed out Cookie Club card that says I have the right to those cookies!

Customized License Plates

Let me be clear; not all of them are bad. I once saw a customized license plate that said 2KWL4SKWL—straightforward, simple, and hilarious. What I can't stand is when a license plate is customized to an inside joke or something personal. Like some girl loves her dog, "Tutu," so she gets a vanity plate that says "ILVToTDG." Then I get behind her and start reading it: I love tot dog? I love to tug? I love...to...duce dog? Then I crash into a school for the blind...and *I'm* the one who goes to jail?! I mean it's hard enough to drive while texting, playing iPhone Scrabble and drinking my coffee. Now I have to figure out your inside joke? Christ. Have some consideration for the other people on the road. It's just not safe. C'mon, use your head.

One time I was driving in California with a girl on a first date. We had just met, and we were stuck in traffic (L.A.) so we were sounding out vanity plates for fun. California loves vanity plates; it's ridiculous. This guy pulls up in front of us with the plate, "OLDNGRN." We were both puzzled for a few moments....

Then suddenly I blurted, "Oh, it's old Nigerian! Look, a Black guy is driving it."

Then my date subtly unblurted, "Actually, I think it's 'old and green.' He's driving a vintage green Mustang."

We didn't say much for the rest of the trip.... I mean, I tried to mention that I was a democrat and talk about how much I love raps to save some face, but it was too late. The damage was done. Thanks a lot, vanity plates.

Unicorns

Listen; if you are like most people...you're Asian. Also, you like unicorns. Well, I happen to think unicorns are the worst. Everyone is always pretending that unicorns are so fascinating, but I think the only reason we like them is because they don't exist. If unicorns had always existed and were at the zoo right now, you wouldn't care at all. In fact, you would ignore your little nephew's pleas to go to the zoo and see them cause *Ice Loves Coco* is on, and you already put Bagel Bites in the oven.

Think about it. Have you ever seen a giraffe? Those things are ten times more fascinating than a horse with a horn on its head! Giraffes are like a Dali painting come to life. They are like nine feet tall with polka dots and black tongues!! Now, when was the last time you went to see a giraffe? If you are any self-respecting adult, you probably go see your dentist more than you admire a giraffe at the local zoo. I imagine God is in heaven all like, *"Unicorns!? Are you fucking kidding me? Have you not seen the giraffes?! I gave you giraffes, you ungrateful dolts!"*

If Unicorns were at the zoo, you would walk right by them, playing on your phone, while stoned teenagers threw pebbles at them. There are white-bellied spider monkeys like ten minutes from my house at the Philadelphia Zoo right now, and I couldn't care less. But if they never existed and someone just made them up, I would love them. I'd be drawing them on my Trapper

Keeper, and using them as the punch line in alternative comedy stand-up routines.

Rooftop Parties

Now I know what you're thinking: *how can you hate a rooftop party, Ryan? Sure, some chips might blow away due to the breeze; but other than that you can party, see a great view and smoke a cigarette without having to catch a plane to the nearest designated smoking area. It's a happening good time!* Well, first of all, who says "happening good time?" What are you like a flapper from the twenties? Stop talking like an idiot. Secondly, I hate rooftop parties because it breaks my #1 rule: do not combine times of social anxiety and easy access to suicide. It's a simple rule. For a guy like me, a rooftop party is like speed dating in a knife store or having a job interview on an eroding highway median. One time I seriously considered putting a fork through my neck just because I accidentally signed the customer copy of the credit card receipt three times in one day. It doesn't take much to get people like me to think this way. If I'm at a killer roof deck party with pretty girls and cool media types, odds are I will say something stupid or bomb a joke, and then, in the heat of the moment, fling myself over the edge of the roof just to end it. In all honesty, I should legally have to leave my belt and shoelaces at home anytime I go out to interact with other people.

I Bet...

I bet..."Where did you register?" is the only phrase you'll hear at both a wedding shower and a sex offender's parole hearing.

I bet...giving people diarrhea is Jesus's favorite guilty pleasure. If you had the power to give people diarrhea, it would be impossible not to do it, just ask Cracker Barrel!

I imagine Jesus and bunch of his angels are hanging out in paradise and looking down like, "Awe, check out this guy: he's in a full tux for his sister's wedding. This is going to be hilarious!"

Then God the Father pops out of a cloud and is like, "Jesus...you are not giving people diarrhea again are you? I told you before; that is not the way it works. It's liquids in the front, solids in the back. Don't make me come in there!"

And Jesus is all, "Um, yeah, Dad. I know. We are just umm...praying." Then he whispers to the angels, "Check out this guy, he just ate all those tacos and he's about to tie his shoes."

Then Jesus and angels laugh and laugh then shush each other so God the Father doesn't hear.

I bet...an invention that would sell really well would be a car that instantly rolls the windows up whenever Shania Twain comes on the radio, so I stop embarrassing myself at stop lights. I'm just saying that would definitely Im-press-a me much!

I bet...the guy who came up with the scoring system for tennis was a real first-class asshole. *"Instead of 0 we are going to say love because it's cute, and instead of 1 point it's 15 points and 2 points are 30 points. But the 3rd point is 40, not 45. Because I said so! It's my game! Also, you need 2 points to win. Now let me explain 'duce' to you."*

I bet...the balk rule in baseball was originally called: The "C'mon don't be a dick, man, just throw the ball already" Rule.

I bet...using a Neti Pot is the closest white people will ever get to being water boarded.

I bet...there are a few girl ghosts that hang outside of female changing rooms in gyms just to stop guy ghosts from having any fun.

I bet...a good field sobriety test for white males would be for the cop to play Billy Joel's "Moving Out" on a boom box, and if the driver can resist singing along, he's free to drive home.

I bet...if you spend over $200 at Michaels; they give you a free cat and a stack of old newspapers for your house.

Girls Girls Girls

Ladies' Man

I'm no ladies' man. I'll be the first to admit it. Sex with me is like an amusement park ride...it's bumpy, repetitive, and it takes an overweight security guard to get me off. To give you a small glimpse into the amount of "swag" I have, I once said, "I really appreciate you doing this," to a girl during sex.

I was denied on various online dating sites for not being "interesting" enough, which is ridiculous because the Philadelphia Police Department has named me a "person of interest" like five times in the last two years.

To be honest, I'm not *completely* inexperienced when it comes to the ladies. One time my dentist brushed her boob on the side of my head during a routine checkup. She later told me that it "meant nothing" and she's "happily married" and added "stop calling my house." But we all know love can make people say some crazy things. Old flames die hard, I guess. I don't know what ever happened to that girl. We lost touch some time ago, and the rumors I've heard through the grapevine are questionable at best. The only thing I can say with any real certainty is that she died in a freak helicopter accident in the Balkans a few summers back.

I also once had a threesome with my girlfriend and her friend. A lot of people said that it didn't count though cause my girl-friend's friend was a dude and my main role in the threesome was operating the video camera, but as my grandmother always said, "haters gonna hate."

Outside of these few impressive incidents, I've always been a disaster when it comes to girls. Girls used to be friends but some-where along the line things got weird and awkward, like that time I parked my Jeep Patriot next to a Jeep Cherokee. I've spent most of my life trying to figure out what happened and exactly when was the moment that everything went wrong...and I finally think I found it. Remember in 5th grade when the teachers took all the girls out of the class and they returned an hour later looking re-ally confused and terrified, carrying little bags with deodorants and things? Now, I don't know what they said during that hour,

I always assumed it was spent teaching the girls things like, "Don't worry about parallel parking, no one will expect you to know how to do it anyway." But, without a doubt this is the moment that everything went wrong between boys and girls. And things just haven't been the same since.

Being good with girls is all a matter of self-confidence, which I've just never had. Except this one time I slammed a Red Bull and listened to an entire Pink CD, but I got pretty sick afterwards, so I didn't get to show off all that confidence I had accumulated. My anxiety around girls has been a life-long battle. For a few months in college, it was so bad that I was diagnosed with that condition where you never leave your house. I think my therapist said it's pronounced, "being a pussy." I've never been the guy who can just approach girls and start a conversation. If a safe word is a word that tells a girl to back off sexually, I think mine might be "hello." I've gotten better in time, and I'm sure one day I'll find the perfect gal for me—someone to start a family with—a soul mate and partner who will raise our kids as respectable, decent people who cut their sandwiches diagonally like civilized human beings.

It's easy to get depressed when you're single, but I mean even Chucky, the enchanted ginger murder doll, found a girl willing to marry him. So to all the single boys and ladies out there, keep the faith! Finding "the one" is not supposed to be easy, but if you do it right, you only have to do it once. It's like Neo in the Matrix, except with slightly less bullet dodging involved, and of course, guy agents aren't following you through phones and stuff. So that part is nice.

Mysterious Guys

Like most boys, I don't know a lot about girls. I don't know if they like being hit on, if size matters, or where they pee out of.... It's a mystery like the Bermuda Triangle. No one knows for sure what's going on down there. Science has yet to crack that puzzle. I'm certainly no Don Juan, so I'm probably not the best person to give advice. But one thing I do know, is girls like mysterious guys. Like next time you are on a blind date show up and hand the girl a snow globe without saying a word. Then be like, "I'm just going to go use the bathroom." but just drive off and never talk to her again. It'll drive her CRAZY.

Sometimes when I'm out on a date and things are getting a little stale, I will pay the waiter $40 to come up to the table and say, "Sorry to interrupt, Mr. White, but *tiramisu* is not on the menu." and then give me a menacing nod.

Then I pause for a second and put a very concerned look on my face. I jump up, punch the waiter in the jaw, flip the table, grab my date by the hand, and say, "They found me! We have to leave now! Follow me." Then we dart out the back door and jump into my car. I swerve out of the parking lot and say, "I'm sorry you have become a part of this, but if you don't do what I say, they'll kill you to get to me."

At this point, her pulse should be racing. I weave in and out of traffic while looking up every couple of seconds like I'm scanning for helicopters. Then I yell, "How do they know about Berlin? Your cell phone, give me your cell phone!" Then I open up the back of her phone and say, "bugged!" and throw it out the window of my Mitsubishi Lancer. Then I'll say something like, "Are you with them? Who sent you here? KGB? CIA? Black Ops? NAACP?"

She will then start crying and exclaim, "No one sent me!" and "I have no idea what is going on!"

Then I pull over under a bridge. I tell her I believe her, and she is the only one I can trust. I give her a pensive yet hopeful look and tell her to meet me in the Marion Hotel under the name Samantha Stone in forty minutes. I mention that it is "a matter of national security." After we bang, I tell her I have to go underground for a few weeks, and tell her she should "lay low" and "stay off the grid" for a while, too. I end the night by saying, "It's too dangerous to take you with me but I'll never forget you."

They usually see me at a Jamba Juice a few weeks later and get really upset, but deep down I bet they probably had a great time.

Bathroom Mirrors

I like my relationships like my jackets...straight and impossible to get out of. When I met my girlfriend this year, I moved in with her almost immediately. One thing I have learned through this experience is that girls love bathroom mirrors. I used to get angry with my girlfriend for taking too long to get ready for family events or parties, but I don't anymore for several reasons. One, it is amazing I even have a girlfriend. Seriously, it's a miracle. When I say, "my girlfriend is off the chain," people usually assume that I mean she has escaped from her shackles in the basement. My high school yearbook quote was, "I'm tired of people assuming I have a small dick just because I drive a Ferrari...it's because I'm Irish." To be fair, I thought it was off the record, even though the guy did say I was definitely on the record several times. The point is: I'm lucky to have a girlfriend.

Another reason I don't get mad when my girlfriend is taking her time in the bathroom is because I think girls are doing more than changing during those times. Now, I'm not 100% positive but I'm pretty sure when they're taking their shirt off they leave it on the top of their head and pretend they have long hair and twirl it like a southern belle or they pretend they're a nun and other weird stuff like that. I have caught my girlfriend in these moments. So, I say, let girls have their playtime, it builds their imaginations. Imaginations are important and can be helpful for sexy role-playing or wanting your girlfriend to pretend she is not dating an idiot.

Excerpts from Diary #3

August 19, 2011

Dear Diary,

I just turned down an acting gig on America's Most Wanted. I figure those actors probably get wrongfully arrested a lot.

September 21, 2011

Dear Diary,

Accidentally sprayed my cat with BOD body spray instead of water this morning and now he's ordering Red Bull and Vodkas and calling things "tight."

September 30, 2011

Dear Diary,

Just read an article that said Chick-Fil-a contributes to anti-gay organizations. New idea: create a pro-gay rights Chick-Fil-a and call it "Chick on Chick-Fil-a."

October 14, 2011

Dear Diary,

I bet if the days of the week were a family, Manic Monday would really resent Lazy Sunday cause everyone would like him better even though he didn't do shit. And Thursday would just be annoying because he would always be "thirsty."

October 18, 2012

Dear Diary,

Comcast called me to schedule an interview for a job I applied for today. I said I would come by sometime between 9:00 a.m. and 4:30 p.m. either Wednesday or Thursday. Strangely, they found that inconvenient.

This and That

Middle School P.I.: The Case of The Red Scare

Of all the snack bars in town, she had to walk into mine.... Last Tuesday passed like any other school day; it was a cool afternoon; the cafeteria served Texas Tommys, and Mrs. Turtello assigned way too much homework on a bunch of stuff we hadn't even gone over yet, which is so unfair. It would seem like any other day at Middlebury Middle School; that is, unless, you were in Mrs. Simmon's algebra class.

At approximately 2:00 p.m., Mrs. K., our health teacher, entered the algebra class and asked all female students to line up and follow her for a "special health class." The girls and boys exchanged confused and suspicious glances—why would just the girls have a "special class?" The teachers looked uncomfortable and awkward—something was clearly afoot. We may have been in algebra class, but something definitely didn't add up. I wanted answers.

Forty minutes later the girls slowly shuffled back into class, each of them with a look of reserved terror on their face. They each carried a small plastic bag filled with what smelled like baby powder and crackled like a bad Christmas wrapping job as it swayed. Clearly, these girls had witnessed something terrible. But what...I couldn't say.

Every girl in the class denied my request for an interview. It seemed the administration had bought their silence with a few bars of soap and some kind of paper string nunchuk thingy. The whole thing stunk to high-heaven, but no one was making a peep. Everyone seemed to be trying to cover it up...like a boner in gym class.

I hit the recess yard in search for answers. Word on the street was this kid, Matt Taner, had a sister in the class, and I had a feeling he knew more than he was letting on. Matt was a typical lowlife 6th grader and was known to spend day and night curled up in the downtown monkey bars. About two years ago he crawled into a juice box, and he hasn't been out since.

When I approached Matt, he told me to scram like an egg. He was as tight-lipped as Kate Carny during Seven Minutes in Heaven. And just like Kate, I could tell Matt wanted nothing to do with me. I figured a package of Funfetti Dunkaroos could get him talking. In my business, it helps to take a page from Teddy Roosevelt: *"Speak softly but carry a big stick."* Only my stick was a pixie stick, guaranteed to get any two-bit punk from these parts to spill his guts like a piñata. Hesitantly, Matt told me I could find his sister at the snack bar of the local pool that Saturday. It had been a long week, and it seemed I was getting more questions than answers. I only hoped this dame wasn't yanking my chain, especially since my chain was connected to my wallet and Jenco jeans.

I knew that pool like the back of my hand and, believe me—as a 7th grade boy—I knew the back of my hand well. Matt's sister was Sarah Taner, a real doll face, with a smile like heaven and right hook that could send ya there—if you didn't play your *Pokémon* cards right. What a broad like her was doing in a dive snack bar like that I'll never know.

She looked me over, put a candy cigarette in her mouth, and said, "I could use a drink."

I slid over a Motts apple juice.

"Anything stronger, sweetheart?" she asked.

I smirked and pulled a Kool-Aid twist off out of my backpack, the real stuff (none of that Mondo bullshit).

She took down half of it in a single gulp, then handed me a slip of paper with numbers on it and said, "I think this will answer your questions, but I'm warning ya, you might not like what you find."

And just like that, she was gone—vanished like a poorly drawn wiener on a shaken etch-a-sketch.

The numbers looked familiar: 331.04136. I know I had seen these kind of numbers before. Then I remembered Mr. Durkin's library class. They were Dewy Decimal numbers. I high-tailed it to the school library.

It only took a few minutes to find it—a thin book with a deceivingly innocent cover—*Are You There God? It's Me, Margaret.* Fitting, I thought God would be the one answering my prayers. It all came together like a disturbing jigsaw puzzle. Page after page revealed the sickening truth and it stung like a dodge ball to the face on a cold afternoon. One thing I've learned in this business is that sometimes the worst thing about a case is finding exactly what you are looking for....

Gross. Seriously, that's gross.

Graph #1

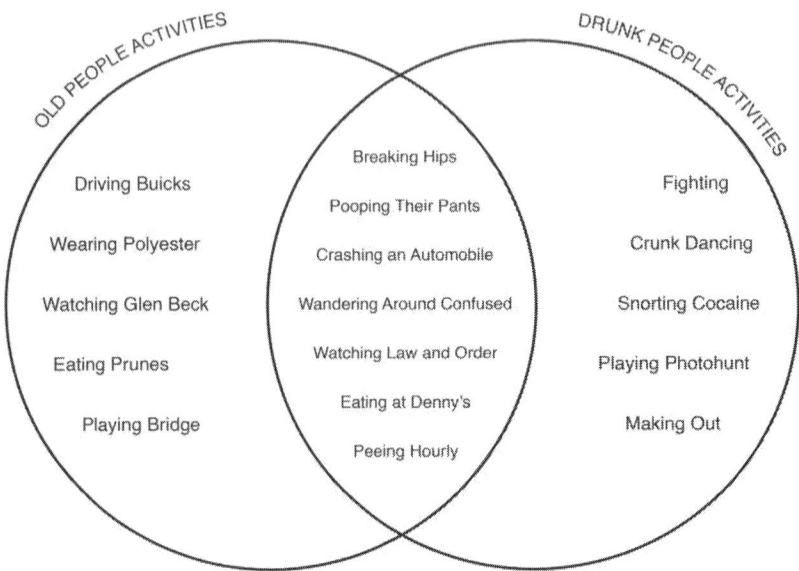

Growing Up Street

People always want to know what it was like to grow up "street." Well I'm here to tell you that having a rough and tough upbringing ain't no picnic. I was raised by a single mother...and a single father. There was just one of each of them; that's just what it was like growing up in my neighborhood. Everyone's family was like that. We never thought anything of it. Things weren't easy. Sometimes the WiFi Internet connection would be out for hours, other times my nanny would be nearly twenty minutes late to pick me up from fencing practice. Heck, I once watched my parents engage in a brutal knife fight in front of my baby sister. It was at Pottery Barn. My mother wanted the seven-piece knife set, but my father didn't think the design went well with the new granite island at our vacation villa. Some harsh words were exchanged. It was ugly...real ugly, but I learned to make do. I believe that how one reacts to dire circumstances is what defines them as a person. I managed to persevere.

I learned the streets quick. Namely Pine St. and Union St. where the junior boys' yacht club was. I ignored my summer reading lists and got an education in the school of hard knocks. Sure, I could have read those books my teachers asked me to, but I didn't need to read some dumb book to know what it was like to be an *Outsider*, or what happens when you feed a mockingbird tequila. I learned by "doing" (stealing a bottle of Don Julio Real from my father's study).

I won't lie. I got into some pretty bad stuff back then. I'm talking about a depraved and twisted game called "ring and run." Yup, I'd walk up to some unsuspecting house, ring the doorbell and then straight run away. That's right, no note or anything! Just rang and then peeled out like a potato in Belfast!

The poor guy answering the door was probably like, "Oh look honey, someone must be at the door, I'll just open it now....Huh? What the heck?!"

Boom! No one is there you idiot, cause I already ran away! Of course, I typically did this around 2:00 p.m. on a weekday afternoon, so most people probably weren't home anyway, but I bet a few moms got awfully red in the face over my blatant disregard for suburban social norms. Again, I can't be entirely sure about that, cause I ran away. That's an integral element to the ring and run thing...the running part. Like I gave an F! I was a cul-de-sac hoodlum who ignored the rules of society—staying up late and illegally downloading Jerky Boy Mp3s with all kinds of curses on them, or prank calling the coach of my sailing team. Am I proud of who I was back then? No. But I did what I had to do to get by until I could find a way out of that neighborhood and into a respectable non-state university and a cushy position at my father's firm.

Are You Smarter than a 5th Grader?
Yes, Yes You Are

Are You Smarter than a 5th Grader is a television show that quizzes adults on 5th grade curriculum. If you lose, which most people do, you are forced to look into the camera and say, "I am not smarter than a 5th grader." I have a real problem with this entire show's premise. They say the 5th grader is "smarter" than you if he answers 5th grade trivia better than you. Of course he's going to have an edge in social studies and basic science; he studies that stuff every day. If you paired an astrophysicist against a barista in a *Name that Coffee* contest, the barista is probably going to win, but it doesn't make him smarter than the astrophysicist.

Let's make it fair. If that 5th grader is so much smarter than me, how bout we test to see who is better at driving a car, or filing taxes, or not getting ripped off by a corner drug dealer in North Philly. Let's see who knows more about talking their way out of a public intoxication ticket at 4:00 a.m. at a Denny's after accidentally peeing on a police dog. Let's see little 5th grade Jimmy take on some of those questions. Hey Jimmy, when your girlfriend says you're drinking too much because she can't handle you having fun when it isn't directly connected to her, how do you respond? Oh, what's that, Jimmy? No answer? Having trouble even wrapping your head around the question? Yeah, that's what I thought. Drink your apple juice and remember you are not smarter than an adult, any adult, even the dumbest inbred syphilitic-brained adult in the world is a rocket scientist compared to you.

Advice to My Unborn Son

In 2009, some guy wrote a book and blog called, *1001 Rules for My Unborn Son* and it got very popular. I read a few of them. At first it was cute, but somewhere around Rule# 500 it seemed pretty overbearing and a bit controlling for a kid who wasn't even born yet. Also, one of his rules was: always show up early. I'm no doctor, but telling an unborn baby to show up early sounds pretty dangerous to me. Premature births are not "basic etiquette," jerk! Anyway this guy got me thinking of some things I've learned in my life that I could share with my future son. Of course, I'm assuming in the future there will be a way to procreate with a gym sock. So I'm taking a bit of a leap, but....

Here are some words of wisdom to my unborn child:

- Always be yourself...unless you are totally lame, then be someone else who is cooler. Cause c'mon no one wants to deal with your lame shit.
- Take it from me, don't make a Grinch joke when you find out your baby cousin was born with a heart three times too small. No one appreciates comedy anymore.

- You should never play with fire...unless you want to look really cool. I mean really, really, cool with sick-ass fireballs and shit!

- Don't grow a mustache, unless you become a cop or a pedophile, then you kinda have to.

- Remember, don't open up a Target in Afghanistan.

- Never send a work email from your phone. If you send an email that says, "Sent from my iPhone," your co-workers will immediately assume you wrote it while you were taking a shit. You might as well write it in brown font!

- If you ever see someone on a plane take out their headphones for a second, concentrate, then put them back in.... They just farted.

- Remember, children are like fruit: they bruise easily, and if you let them out of the cupboard for too long they get spoiled.

- Don't yell "five second rule!" after you drop a baby.

- Getting your stepfather a #2 Dad coffee mug is a hurtful Father's Day present. I learned this the hard way.

- The excuse, "don't kill the messenger" doesn't work if you are convicted of mailing a bunch of people Anthrax.

- Saying, "You have the sex appeal of a woman half your age," is a sexy thing to say to a forty-five-year-old woman, but a really creepy thing to say to a twenty-six-year-old woman.

- Remember son, girls may say they want a guy who will cuddle with them, but this does not include the girl who falls asleep on the subway.
- Never name your child, "Marco" on the off chance he is kidnapped at a public pool.

  You: Marco?!

  Everyone Else: Polo!
- It's called a food court cause if you eat there, you are giving the world permission to judge you.
- Remember son, it's easier to childproof your girlfriend than it is your apartment.
- "Funnel cake" is delicious if it's a noun, and gross and dangerous if it's a verb.
- The poster, "You miss 100% of the shots you don't take," is a poor choice for decorating the Alcoholics Anonymous room.
- If you are giving 110% of yourself to be good at something, you will succeed...unless it's basic mathematics.
- Having a "bottomless margarita" special at your bar will bring in customers. Having a "bottomless Shirley Temple" special at your bar will bring in the wrong kind of customers...and probably child protection services.
- "The way to a man's heart is through his stomach" is great advice for new lovers and horrible advice for new surgeons.
- Indian Summer is a way better wedding theme than Arab Spring.

- "Gay clubbing" is a fun night in NYC, and a hate crime in Alabama.

- Every chocolate cake is a Death by Chocolate Cake if you're a diabetic or a dog.

- Don't go around calling broads "dames." Skirts hate that kind of talk.

- Always be wary of a girl who is not a doctor, but knows how to spell Chlamydia correctly.

- Don't order the sizzling Fajitas at Chilies. If you need attention that bad, go join a band or write a comedy book.

- On the "Poor Life Decisions" scale, owning a Bluetooth falls somewhere between graduate school and being a Juggalo.

- Having coffee with someone is a good way to learn more about them...specifically whether or not they have Irritable Bowel Syndrome.

- Never take advice from a guy with a wrist tattoo. (Also, never get a wrist tattoo.)

- If you keep your Tamagotchi pet alive for too long, it gets weird. Mine is now talking about grad school and needs money for an abortion.

- When in Rome do as the Romans do...start a really big fire then blame it on Christians.

- Never run from your problems, especially if one of your problems is asthma.

- Showers are like baths except you can pee while taking one without it being gross.

- If you say the word "hater" more than twice a week, you are probably the problem

- It's all fun and games until someone loses an eye...then it's an awesome story you have about your friend's EYE FALLING OUT!!

- Always be sure to check the warning label on fireworks...the bigger it is, the more fun that thing will be to play with.

- Going streaking as an eighty-year-old woman isn't "right" or "wrong," it's a grey area—a big disgusting grey area.

- It's not whether you win or lose...it's whether I win or lose, that's important.

- True beauty comes from the inside...so swallow a tapeworm.

- All you need is love...unless you are taking your little nephew camping then you definitely need his insulin medication too. Lesson learned.

- Honesty is a great strategy when ending a relationship...but so is FIRE!

- Blog like no one's watching. P.S.: No one IS watching.

- FamilyWatchdog.us is THE WORST dating website.

- Any nickname becomes instantly cooler if it's in Spanish or begins with El. For example, if your nickname is Teapot (and this is just a hypothetical), you'd be El Tetera. Pretty cool.

- Listen son, don't judge a book by its cover. Or its contents. Real men don't read books. Books are for nerds.

- People who scapegoat other people are the reason for all of our problems.

- The worst question you can ask a potential employer in an interview is probably, "why are you hitting yourself?! Huh?"

- Give a man a phish and he'll be gross for a day, teach a man to phish, and he's gross for a lifetime.

- Münchausen Syndrome has nothing to do with German lesbians.

- Blood is thicker than water...so use that when making your pasta sauce...I guess.

- Being against the sexual objectification of women is a good way to score smoking hot tail.

- Keeping your lift ticket on your ski jacket is a good way to let people know you are a piece of garbage.

- Trying to become a standup comedian is like cutting without all the mess.

- Never get involved with Fundamental Evangelicals and people into CrossFit.

- You can yell at your husband/wife for snoring, even if they don't snore, and they can't really do anything about it. Seriously, you can smack them in the face when they are sound asleep, yell at them, and they will probably just apologize to you.

- If you see Christina Aguilera in a bottle don't let her out. Trust me, just leave her in there.

- Romance Tip: Surprise her with the Jaws theme or some carnival music in your next sex playlist to creep her out real good.

- You can take the girl out of the city, but you can't take the girl's dog...cause that's stealing and it's gonna be a "whole thing."

- If your girlfriend asks you to hold her purse, be sure to grip it in a fist and hold it like a decapitated head. Like, *"look how totally straight I am! I don't even know how this thing works!"*

- If you ever eat Bugles *without* putting them on your fingers like a spooky witch, then you should just go ahead and join Al-Qaeda already.

- Drugs are not the answer...unless the question is, "what is not the answer?" Then yeah, I guess drugs are the answer.

- When hitting on a pretty girl, tell her she is like a beautiful, picked flower. Also leave out the whole "cause you'll be dead in a week" part.

- If you open up a gay gym a good name for it would be, "Build-A-Bear Workshop."

- Wearing a keyboard tie to a murder trial is a good way to let the jury know, "Yeah, I killed my wife...but not my sense of humor."

Excerpts from Diary #4

October 17, 2011

Dear Diary,

My vacation in Hawaii has been going well but something strange happened today. I was at the bar enjoying a julep, when I noticed this beautiful woman staring at me from across the bar. She waited till she had my attention then put a cherry stem in her mouth and tied it into a knot using just her tongue. The message was clear—she would twist my dick into a painful knot if she ever got the chance.

I ran as fast as I could.

November 12, 2011

Dear Diary,

My friend threw a Victorian-themed party and requested everyone wear period clothing. I showed up in my girlfriend's loose gray sweatpants and her XL "Franky Says Relax" T-shirt with the ice cream stains on it. They asked me to leave, which was fine because I wasn't "technically" invited, and I was feeling crampy anyway.

December 30, 2011

Dear Diary,
My step dad invited me to come downstairs to his dinner party and play Wii Tennis tonight. They gave me the remote, and I played pretty intensely for an hour and a half before I realized there was no game and they had just turned on an actual tennis match on TV. I should have known that most people don't laugh that hard during a Wii Tennis Match.

July 1, 2011

Dear Diary,
I think Ikea stands for Impoverished Kids Emulating Adults.

Campfire Stories

Panic Attack at the Disco

I was just at a party telling some great stories and making everyone laugh and pay attention to me, then this clumsy kid with hemophilia fell down the steps and totally RUINED it. Everyone was like, "Call an ambulance!" right before my big punch line. It's like, way to go and mess the night up for everyone with your self-centered accident. Anyway, when everyone was helping the paramedics and catering to this colossal idiot, I had the dance floor all to myself. Now I've never been much of a dancer per say—having an anxiety disorder usually means you are not going to be cutting a rug—but it got me thinking there should be some dance moves that those of us with crippling anxiety can master.
So I invented some:

1. **The Running Man**: You see a social situation and then you run from it as quickly as possible.

2. **The Tango**: Nervously approach a group of cute girls dancing, then accidentally spill your drink on your crotch as you try to talk to them and watch the *tang-go* right out the door.

3. **The Worm**: Agree to dinner and dancing plans with your friends Mark and Sara early on in the week, then worm your way out of it at the last second and watch *The Craft* on TV while eating pizza rolls.

4. **The Pop and Lock**: Pop a Valium and Lock your bedroom door.

5. **The Electric Slide**: When someone says, "Hey, let's dance." you discretely turn the lights off then "slide" out the back door when no one can see. When your friends text you later, make something up about someone dying.

An Excerpt from My Gay Cowboy Novel

It was half past noon when Mark and I entered the dusty bar that smelled of tobacco smoke and spilled whiskey. This was the fifth bar we had been to that day, and we did not seem to be any closer to finding what we were searching for.

Mark waved over the barkeep—a grizzly man with a salt and pepper beard—and said, "We're looking for Magic Candy Island. Can you point us in the right direction?"

The hefty bartender cracked a smile. "I s'pose a place like that is anywhere you want it to be."

This was the same answer four previous bartenders had offered us.

Mark closed his eyes for a second and then exploded. "Well, if that was true, I wouldn't have to ask for fucking directions would I!"

As Mark cursed and yelled, I shot him the "We are gay, let's not yell" look, and then quickly pulled him out of the bar. Our silver penis-shaped spurs jingled loudly as we walked back to our horses.

Defeated, we began the journey home. We returned to our campgrounds only to find our horse troughs mysteriously filled with candy corn.

We were close...very close.

My New Edgy Sitcom

Lately, I've been writing some scripts to break into the world of TV writing. I've got a few projects in the pipeline right now. I'm making a *Sex in the City* spin-off/crime drama. It's either going to be called *Miranda Rights* or *License to Carrie*. I haven't decided yet, but it's going to be huge. Comedy writing is tough though. Let's face it, comedy sitcoms are no good these days. I've seen funnier plots in a children's cemetery. Hey-O! But don't worry, I'm writing this really sweet sitcom to pitch to the networks full of some hi-larious stuff that I wanted to tell you guys about. Like there's this one scene where my brothers and I ask our mom which one of us she loves the most and she responds, "It's a tie...for last place!" (Studio audience goes nuts.) It's full of super edgy stuff like that.

There will be a scene where a poisonous snake bites my upper thigh, and my friend has to suck the poison out, but he's all hesitant to because he doesn't want to appear to be a homosexual! LOLZ! Ya know, because men would rather have their friends die than do something that kind of looks similar to something a gay person would do. That's comedy! Basically, anything about being scared to look gay is comedy gold. Oh man, I'm in stitches just thinking about it.

Also, we're going to insert the word "bro" into other words a lot. Like a girl will ask my character, "Are you pro-life?" and I'll respond, "I'm bro-life." Then I will high-five the one Black guy friend I have on the show, whom I will have a...wait for it...wait for it..."bromance" with. LOL! Bro is also comedy gold.

Most of this "hip irreverent comedy" will focus around me and my best friend's relationship. The relationship will run the spectrum from "it's funny cause they are guys and have almost a couples-type relationship," to "it's funny because they are uncomfortable in situations that may be misconstrued as gay because they have a couples-type relationship." LOLZ! (Ya know, almost like they are gay, but we know they're definitely not gay from all the poon they slay!)

Put on your laughing hats folks, it's going to be a real chuckle fest!

Civil War Letters

You would think a civil war would be a good thing, or at least, a lesser evil war than all the other wars we just call "war." If you're going to have a war, you should be civil about it, right? —A war in which people may disagree but are still respectful of one another's feelings and stuff? Well, it turns out civil wars are not civil at all, not by a long shot. When I was younger, my parents used to take my brothers and me to the old civil war fields around Brandywine and Gettysburg, Pennsylvania for battle reenactments. My parents were not particularly into history or war stuff; I'm not really sure how this became a tradition. They probably took us there to relax and were secretly hoping to see one of us get trampled by a spooked horse that got away from the Union Colonel—who actually works at the cell phone kiosk at the mall.

One thing I do love about civil war history is the letters soldiers wrote to their wives and sweethearts back home. They were always so eloquent and romantic. Great letter writing is truly becoming a lost art, like calligraphy, writing in cursive or sexism. I couldn't imagine writing letters so beautiful these days. For one, without Spellcheck, my letters would look like a cryptogram that a dyslexic serial killer would send to the head cop investigating the case. Also, texts and emails have built an unshakable foundation in emoticons, slang, and acronyms that have butchered any sense of proper grammar that I once had. Here is how I imagine a civil war letter may read if email was around in the 1860's:

May 10, 1863, Year of Our Lord.

My Dearest Annabelle,
It has been a long time since I had the opportunity of writing to you, and I gladly avail myself of the present opportunity. I am not certain that I will have a chance of sending this, but I will write a few lines. :(
We have been on a raid into the mountains. but I have not the time to give you the particulars of our journey. We captured a good many prisoners while in Montana. and killed a good many 2. LolZ! It was quite an epic pawnage! We fought them nearly all day at the Cape on Sunday, two weeks ago today. The yanks boasted that we would never get back to our base, but they were badly mistaken, what a bunch of noobs!! For we are back again and have sustained but very light loss. :-D It was a great sight—watching them retreat, due to our firm resolve.
I am in hopes that I will get a whole package of letters from you in a few days. I never wanted to see you half as bad in all my life as I do now, FML!! I would give anything in the world to see

you and the children. I have no idea when I will have that pleasure. :'-(

My love and a thousand kisses to my own, sweet Annabelle and our little boys. How my heart yearns for thou that are so near and dear to me. Goodbye my own, sweet wife, for the present. <3

As ever,
Your Devoted and Loving Husband. L8R!

P.S. Send me some nudzzz! LOL!

Excerpts from Diary #5

July 27, 2013

Dear Diary,

I went to my therapist today after work. I wanted to tell her about my inferiority complex but my inferiority complex probably isn't as good as her other patients' inferiority complexes.

July 29, 2011

Dear Diary,

Kim Kardashian just announced that she has been diagnosed with the skin condition psoriasis. This means that after having a sex tape with Brandy's little brother leaked to the world, having a father who acquitted OJ Simpson of murder, and creating a pop song that was deemed "the worst song of all time," there is finally something that can turn her face red.

August 10, 2013

Dear Diary,

Went to the doctor today. Turns out I have a small kidney infection. My doctor said everything should be okay but to monitor my urine, it should look like Gatorade. Just checked and it's a dead ringer for Fierce Grape, so we are good!

October 1, 2013

Dear Diary,

I just got back from my brother's wedding. He asked me to be an Usher but then got all mad when I showed up dancing in black-face and singing "You Got It Bad." It's like make up your mind, man.

Working on Me

The Plight of the Skinny-Fat

My entire life I have been embarrassingly skinny. Imagine Jimmy Fallon with a devastating case of SARS—that kind of skinny. Growing up, I had a physique that could only be described as that of a preteen Filipino gymnast. My fatter friends would always say, "You're lucky now, but wait till your metabolism slows down, you'll see." Well, in the last year I've gained thirty pounds. Thirty pounds! I looked it up; that is the weight of a 14-foot canoe or an average human's legs. So essentially, it's as if I'm carrying around a canoe or have four legs at all times. But I'm actually slower on both land and water. I don't know how this happened. My diet isn't that bad. I only eat food fresh from the farm (Boone's and Pepperidge). Who would have thought that empty calories would weigh so much? My metabolism was supposed to slow down gradually, you know, like a laptop infected with spyware. Instead, it screeched to a halt like a laptop infected with a can of Coke. My metabolism was supposed to slowly fade into obscurity, not abruptly die overnight. It was supposed to be an Andy Rooney. Instead it was a Heath Ledger. No one saw it coming until it was too late.

I first noticed my new found pounds thanks to my Tempur-Pedic bed. (You know, the memory foam beds made from NASA material.) I just kept sinking further and further into the bed. In the beginning, it was just a few subtle centimeters, but now it's ridiculous. I've sunk down so far into the bed that I draw in all the stuff that's on the bed like a whirlpool every night. By the time I wake up, all the things that were on the bed are now on top of me, which means I wake up buried in Toblerone wrappers[3], bank receipts, loose change, and my collection of artisan Thai-made boy dolls, which aren't so much dolls as action figures you dress up in little outfits. Lots of guys are into them, okay? It's not a big deal. Just let it go. Okay just forget I said anything about the dolls. I no longer let my dog sleep in my bed. I keep imagining my poor Boston Terrier in the middle of the night desperately

---

3 A Toblerone is a fancy crispy chocolate bar made with honey…it's essentially a gay Nestle Crunch bar.

clawing and scratching uphill, fighting a losing battle with gravity as he falls towards me backwards like he's being sucked into a wormhole. At this rate I'm going to need my girlfriend to extend a broom or rope to pull me out of the bed like Indiana Jones caught in quicksand. A friend suggested I try flipping the mattress but then it'd be like sleeping on a hill. This would create a whole Humpty Dumpty-like situation, which seems way more dangerous.

Coming to terms with my new found fatness has not been easy...and I have yet to embrace exercise as a friend. Incorporating crunches into my daily life that are not Nestlé in nature seems nearly impossible. People that are skinny and get fat are not fat in the same way as people born fat. People who are born fat are round, like a beanbag, which can be charming in a jolly butterball kind of way. Skinny people who get fat, get "weird fat." I am weird fat. I am not round. I look like a laundry bag stuffed with cardboard boxes. Some areas have stayed skinny while others have gotten fat. Shapes just jut out and protrude from me like a poorly constructed snowman or a figure in Tetris (if your directional buttons were broken). I don't have curves like other bigger people, which stinks because I happen to think curves are super sexy. (My girlfriend has scoliosis.)

Being skinny-fat is also awful because you cannot even complain about it. If a skinny-fat person calls himself fat, actual fat people will despise that person, and they would be right to do so. It's like complaining about the horrors of war when you're still in basic training. It's like walking into a cancer survivors support group and talking about how you "beat cancer" cause you had an abnormal mole removed. It's not cool. Your skinny-fat cross is yours to bear. It will greatly affect your life, but it's not serious enough for anyone to care about. It's not like an eating disorder...except that, I'm probably gonna eat dis-order of fries and probably another. LOL!

But seriously, us skinny-fat people are an underrepresented minority in our culture; lost in a limbo between obesity and healthy living; outcasts to both the fit and the fat. So this weekend, as you shove piles of food down your gullet like a ravenous seagull at the dump, I ask you to remember these sweaty-breasted men doing trust falls into pepperoni pizzas...men who have been deserted by almost everyone.

Mmmmm...deserted; that sounds delicious.

No Shave November

It's a hard fact to face, but we live in a very trying and depressing time. The world is full of suffering, poverty, and injustice. Just the other day I saw a poster that said, *Muscular Dystrophy: Race for the Cure* and it made me really sad. If I had the cure, I would just give it to them. Making sick people race for the cure seems really cruel and unfair. How far can a kid run when he's got muscular dystrophy anyway? What kind of monster creates a race like that? It's heartbreaking.... But hey, that's the world we live in. Thanks, Obama!

84

I have never been someone who has been into performing volunteer services or contributing to others in need. One time I accidentally turned all my white dress shirts pink in the wash and then tried to play it off like it was a breast cancer awareness thing at work, but people saw through that pretty quickly. I'm just not an altruistic person. I refused to sign up for my company's 401k because I thought it was a race for charity or something lame like that. I thought "Ira Roth" was that Jewish kid in marketing who needed the liver transplant operation. No thank you!

I'm at an age now where a lot of my friends create charity events for illnesses or other causes, but it's never like "Watch a Movie for Cancer" or "Beer Pong for Poverty." It always has to be a push-up competition or a triathlon. When this happens I get super depressed. First of all, I am reminded that awful diseases are out there affecting people I love. Secondly, I am reminded how insanely lazy and out of shape I am. I absolutely despise physical exercise. One time this lady next to me at a crosswalk thought I was about to go jogging because it looked like I was doing all these leg stretches and lunges while waiting for the light to change, but really I was dealing with the effects of buying cheap toilet paper. I think that's the closest I ever came to jogging. Tons of my friends run marathons now. My Facebook timeline is just a collage of bloody-nippled friends who just "crushed" their personal best in some triathlon. I realize I will never be that person. The only thing I really have in common with marathon runners is that we both accept the fact that there is a possibility we will lose control of our bowels out in public. For serious runners, it's a result of extreme physical exhaustion. For me, it's usually seeing a scary zombie movie bus ad or a dog without a leash right after Del Taco. Anyway, this is why I like November.

In November, several charities stage No-shave November. During No-shave November, men are encouraged not to shave for the whole month for charity. Now this is an event I can finally get behind! This charity event does not force me to perform any physical exercise, and furthermore, it actually rewards my laziness. I think more charities should follow suit. How about, "Sleeping in for Parkinson's?" Just imagine it. "Sorry, I'm four hours late to work, boss...I just care too much." I would no longer be an unkempt underachiever; I'd be a goddamn philanthropist! How about, "Stop Paying Your Bills for Crohn's Disease." I don't even know if Crohn's disease is a thing anymore or if it's already been cured like Polio or bisexuality, but I'm not going to take the time to look it up. This isn't because I'm lazy, but because I've taken a pledge to "Do Nothing to End World Poverty." It's the least I can do...literally.

No-shave November understands that nothing says you care like an outward sign of absolutely not caring. Like Gandhi said, "Be the opposite of the change you want to see in the world...and make your Facebook photo the picture of a ribbon or something. Problem solved." I'm paraphrasing, but you get it....

So, put down those razors boys and hit the snooze button because not caring is the new caring and the world cannot afford for you to sit around...and NOT do nothing.

Quotes

One of the cool things about writing a book—besides all the cool delusions that materialize about a future filled with lucrative creative writing career endeavors—is that people can then quote all the cool stuff you said and put your quotes in their AOL IM Away Messages (or whatever the kids are using to spy on each other with these days). Then everyone thinks you're really smart and funny and inspirational. Well, to help facilitate that process I decided to pre-package some original quotes for you to spread all around the web in an effort to make me super famous.

Now a lot of people said having a chapter where you quote yourself in your own book is the most conceited, egomaniacal thing they ever heard of.... But when you think about it, a lot of people are left-handed too, and that doesn't make them correct. I mean a lot of people supported Hitler! Were they right? So, all you south-pawed, Hitler-loving people out there calling me an egomaniac can keep your opinions to yourself and spend your time on more important things—like trying to find a Nazi-themed can opener you can operate. Sorry, guys, I got a little heated there. It's just like; left-handed people always want to make it all about them and their support of Hitler, who in my opinion, was just wrong. Why should I listen to people who can't play regular guitars and supported the systematic slaughter of six million Jews? I'm sorry, I cannot and will not do that. So, here are some quotes from me *and by me* that I graciously condensed into a single chapter of a book I wrote *about me* for *you* to enjoy:

"I think most people wave their hands in the air cause they just DO care. Like people drowning in the ocean or fans that want a free T-shirt at a basketball game." – Me, to the kids with the cool backwards hats outside the North Philly youth YMCA, who told me I "best be out," which I think means like "we respect you" or something like that.

"Vodka tonics are a lot like my Facebook page in that they are hidden at work, and constantly refreshing." – Me, to my boss after getting hammered at the company party.

"Life is a lot like golf in the sense that the more strokes you have, the bigger your handicap is...and also it can be pretty sexist." – Me, to the mini-golf security guy who kicked me out for trying to drink the blue colored waterfall again.

"I like my relationships like my bootleg liquor: dirty, danger-ous, and with no labels on it." – Me, to this nun at my cousin's school who muttered something in Spanish with the word "el diablo" in it, which I think means hot wings or something.

"I wonder if people do the wave at water polo matches...seems dangerous." – Me, to the lady at Starbucks who said, "There is no such thing as a businessman-sized coffee."

"So to recap: Ben Franklin flies a kite in a thunderstorm, gets electrocuted, and he's a genius. But I essentially do the same thing by taking my laptop into the shower to finish a game of Snood, and the guy at the Apple Store calls me an idiot." – Me, to my little cousin's 4th grade history class while subbing.

"I bounced around the foster care system a little before being adopted. My mom likes to say that my brother was a gifted child, and I was a re-gifted child." – Me, to the bus lady who said, "You can't pull the chord just to talk."

"When it comes to women, I've always had the pick of the litter. And by that I mean, I usually had to pick them out of actual litter and garbage." – Me, to the lady at Target, who said her line was closed.

"I'm the king of make-up sex...in that I'm really good at making up stories where people actually have sex with me." – Me, to any woman willing to give me the full 30 seconds at this speed-dating event.

Excerpts from Diary #6

October 12, 2011

Dear Diary,

I just had an argument with the girlfriend. Sometimes I wish I could set her to "vibrate." I'm sure she wishes she could set me to "vibrate" too, but for completely different reasons.

October 18, 2011

Dear Diary,

My girlfriend is really into playing doctor. That's when I complain, she kinda ignores me, then she tells me to put my shirt back on and takes most of my money.

October 19, 2011

Dear Diary,

I feel like the only thing really rich musicians and homeless men have in common is that they both poop on buses a lot.

October 20, 2011

Dear Diary,

Someone told me that there was "a special place in hell" for people like me. I couldn't help but feel a little flattered. It's like, am I famous in hell?

Yeah, I am probably famous.

Group Therapy

The Utah Jazz Picks its Team Name

Coach: Okay guys, gather around. We have got some major news. New Orleans has decided to move their professional basketball team here to Utah. So I'd like to welcome you all to the next great professional basketball team, The Utah...Jazz!

Player: Coach, that's great and all but do we have to be the "Jazz," it just doesn't seem that intimidating.

Coach: Listen guys, I know it's not as cool sounding as the "Spurs" or "Colonials," but it's not like "Jazz" is some boring, lame white guy music. It's a hip new dangerous thing in smoky bars where dangerous minorities hang out and do drugs. C'mon, it's edgy! It's not like they are playing jazz at dentists' offices or elevators, or when you are on hold with an operator. Haha! The day that happens, you can call me an idiot! (Everyone laughs.)

Plus the commissioner is not going to let in teams with crazy aggressive names. It's a conservative sport. You don't see anyone out there called the Machine Guns or the Earthquakes or anything. (And everyone laughs again.) Sure, if there were teams out there with ridiculous names like the Raptors, or the fucking Wizards, or the Grizzlies...the Utah Jazz would look pretty fucking stupid by comparison, but that is not going to happen. Trust me. We can't just pick a name like the Timberwolves as a team name. That is ridiculous! Think how the 76ers would feel. Listen, it could be worse. We could be The Nuggets. At least "The Jazz" is never followed by the words "of shit" in normal conversation. So pick those heads up. I'm sure the Utah Jazz will be a cool name for a long, long time.

Family

My family is from New York, but my immediate family lives in, or around, Philadelphia. There has always been a bit of a rivalry between my immediate and my extended family when it comes to football. I'm not a huge sports guy. Don't get me wrong, I really like football; I'm just not a big fan of all the tackling and ball throwing. But other than that, I think it's great.

About two years ago the New York Giants beat the Philadelphia Eagles in a heartbreaking game. In the last minute, Eli Manning chucked a Hail Mary pass and connected in the end zone for a devastating win. When the Giants won, my uncle called my parents' house, disguised his voice and left a voicemail saying, "Hey, this is Eli Manning. Sorry about what happened to your boys in Philadelphia. I bet their asses are sore as hell. See ya, losers!"

My mother does not watch football and has literally no idea who Eli Manning is. She listened to the message and then...she panicked. She thought my brother and I, who lived in Philadelphia, were molested by some strange man named Eli Manning. I received a frantic voicemail: "Ryan, this is your mother. Call me immediately. Eli Manning called the house and left a threatening message. I am very worried!"

I called her back and she immediately asked, "Who is Eli Manning?" Still upset about the close game I jokingly said, "Eli Manning is a shit quarterback." My mom gasped and then quietly said, "Oh, my God.... What does that mean?!"

I never really clarified this with my mother, but I'm pretty sure she thought, "shit quarterback" was slang for a guy who likes to molest kids or something. And when I think about it "shit quarterback" is a great term for someone who molests people. It just fits.

Holden Caulfield Visits a Career Counselor

Career Counselor: Hi Holden, I am a career counselor. I'm here to help you find what occupation you might want to pursue based on your personality. Now I noticed on your intake form you wrote, "Catcher" under preferred occupation. I assume you mean like a professional baseball player?

Holden: No. I mean like if all these kids are playing in this big field of rye, and I'm standing on the edge of some crazy cliff, what I have to do is I have to catch everybody if they start to go over the cliff—I mean if they're running and they don't look where they're going I have to come out from somewhere and catch them. That's all I'd do all day. I'd just be the catcher in the rye and all.

Career Counselor: Oh. O...kay.

Holden: That is the only thing I could imagine doing.

Career Counselor: Well I have to say Holden, traditionally schools or other recreational groups for children do not put soccer fields or play yards next to "crazy cliffs." So, I'm thinking that the demand for that kind of thing might be low.

Holden: Bunch of phonies, if you ask me.

Career Counselor: Maybe, or maybe your number one career aspiration is to be a type of human fence in a scenario that would only exist in the hallucinations of a dying pedophile, but let's not lose focus here. Perhaps you could channel your love for tackling small children into a career in concert security for One Direction or something?

Holden: I was also thinking about the lagoon, down near Central Park South. I was wondering where the ducks went when the lagoon gets all icy and frozen over. I wondered if some guy came in a truck and took them away to a zoo or something. Maybe I could be that guy?

Career Counselor: ...Wow. Yeah, I really didn't think you could say something dumber than the whole child catcher thing but...there it is. Holden, have you considered a career with Panera Bread?

The Wu-Tang Clan Picks Their Names

Method Man: We will be the first nine member rap crew with the illest rhymes and the illest names. So far we got me; the Method Man, Raekwon, Ghostface Killah, Inspectah Deck, U-God, Masta Killa and Ol' Dirty Bastard. These names are crazy sick yo. Robert, it's your turn to choose a name.

Robert: Yeah, I've been giving this some thought, and my name will be The RZA.

Method Man: Ooh! That is sick yo. RZA! Good one! Now, it's Gary's turn. Gary, you're the last member to pick a name. What is the killer name you came up with?

Gary: You guys are going to love this one. You can all call me...The GZA!!

Method Man: GZA?

Gary: Yeah, GZA. Sick right?

Method Man: Well...Robert kinda just chose RZA and that's like the same name.

Gary: Umm I don't think so... I said, "GZA with a G." G for Great Name. RZA is with an R. Totally different name.

(Everyone shakes their heads and looks annoyed)

Gary: What??

Method Man: Gary...I'm just going to say it. It kind of seems like you couldn't come up with a name, so you just added the first letter of your real name to RZA. Is that what happened?

Gary: What?? No!! I was thinking about GZA all day, yo! For real!

Method Man: Well on the piece of paper in front of you wrote down the name "Rhyme-guy" a bunch of times. Was that the real name you were going to choose?

Gary: ....

Method Man: Gary, be honest?

Gary: Fine!! Yes it was. You happy, yo? I feel like such a dummy. Rhyme-guy just seemed really lame after all of your super cool names. I was embarrassed, so I panicked. I feel so stupid now!

Method Man: It's okay, Gary. You can be GZA. We are more than just rappers...we're friends. And friendship, well that ain't nothing ta fuck wit.

The Sugar Hill Gang's First Band Meeting

(The members of the Sugar Hill Gang: Wonder Mike, Big Bank Hank, and Master Gee sit down around a table.)

Wonder Mike: Wow guys, we just recorded our first big rap song, "Rapper's Delight." I'm so excited to hear it. The sound engineer is piecing together each of our parts now. My verse is all about how music can bring together people of all different cultures; the black, the white, the red, the brown, the purple, and the yellow. Haha! That's a wholesome and positive message that everyone can embrace!

Master Gee: That sounds great, Mike. My verse is about how I'm one of a kind, and what it's like eating at a friend's house, when their parents' food isn't so great. Like when the chicken tastes like wood! Haha. So you run out the door to buy some antacid but then you call your buddy up later and he says that he understands about the food and not to worry, cause you two are still friends! So everything turns out just fine. A story we can all relate to. What about you, Hank? What's your verse about?

Hank: Well I talk about watching the Knicks play basketball on my color TV...and then it's mainly about me fucking Lois Lane.

Wonder Mike: (choking on drink) ...I'm sorry, Hank. It sounded like you just said your verse is about fucking Lois Lane.

Hank: Yeah, that's right. It's all about me calling her boyfriend, Superman, a "fairy" and then I bang her in a hotel, a motel and a Holiday Inn....

Wonder Mike: SAY WHAT!!! Jesus Christ, Hank! What are you thinking?? You don't literally say "bang her" in the song do you??

Hank: No, I'm not an idiot...I don't say, "bang her." I say, "bust her out with my super sperm."

Wonder Mike: Super sperm?! SUPER SPERM!! What is the matter with you?!?!

Hank: (humping the air) I go do it, I go do it, I go do it, do it, do it, do it....

Wonder Mike: What the hell are you talking about?! Our careers are over, Hank!! I'm going to kill you!!

Excerpts from Diary #7

April 6, 2012

Dear Diary,

I had a dream I was playing in a water-park last night. Now that's what I call a wet dream!! LOL! (Because I ejaculated during it.)

April 7, 2012

Dear Diary,

My doctor said I needed to eat more vegetables, so I started ordering my martinis with two olives. I guess I'm a health freak or whatever now.

April 10, 2012

Dear Diary,

Note to self: Empty cat food cans make great bird feeders...also try not to be so lonely!

April 20, 2012

Dear Diary,

My boss told me he liked my conviction today, which was cool. I didn't realize he knew about those assault charges.

April 26, 2012

Dear Diary,

I made a big step today. I called my stepdad, "Dad." He instantly corrected me though. Whatever! I don't want to watch "1000 Ways to Die" with him anyway. I hate Spike TV, and I hate him!

February 5, 2014

Dear Diary,

A reporter covered an article I wrote in the newspaper today. After like every quote he wrote "(Sic)."

Yeah, that story was sick, bro!

Reflections

Everyone/No One Is Irish on St. Paddy's

This section is about St. Patrick's Day, and while I do not hold an advanced degree in Irish culture or history, I have seen five of the six Leprechaun movies...so I think I know what I'm talking about.

St. Patrick's Day can be a strange day for Irish people. Sure, everyone wants to be Irish when it means slamming back shots of Jameson and making out with a hot redhead. But what about the hard times? Where were these guys during the potato famine? I bet they weren't even around! Well for the Irish frustrated with all these fair-weather fans on St. Patrick's Day, I've got some good news: St. Patrick's Day. Is. A. Lie.

It's true. St. Patrick is famous for driving snakes, and apparently tanning booths and non-boiled food out of Ireland. But the real St. Patrick wasn't even Irish. He was a British-born aristo-crat, and March 17th is the anniversary of his death. So really, St. Paddy's day is a day when the Irish cheer and celebrate for the death of a fancy Englishman, which historically, makes a lot of sense.

St. Patrick's name wasn't even Patrick, it was Succat. Interesting note: many Irishmen still use his name as a type of Irish greeting. You may have heard this name shouted out at an Irish bar or a Boston sporting event. I once wore a Phillies jersey to a Red Sox game and found many of my fellow countrymen greeting me with, "Succat you queer!", "Phillies can Succat,", and other festive variations of this Emerald Isle saying as they show-ered me in beer. The Irish are a very welcoming bunch.

Even the idea of the jolly, sprite, and lucky leprechaun that we so commonly see on St. Paddy's day is a made up myth. In real Irish folklore, leprechauns are actually mean, frail, little shoemakers. They share more in common with today's Indonesian child-labor force than the cartoon mascot for Lucky Charms. They're tragically malicious!

Alright, now that we've established that St. Paddy's day has nothing to do with being Irish, let's get down to what this holiday is really about—drinking till your liver is the size and consistency of Adele's thigh. For all the Irish and non-Irish alike, here are some tips to get you through this mess of a day:

Don't Drink at Your Local Pub

For me, going to a bar is a lot like late-night internet sessions. At first, I causally look around and then I end up opening way too many tabs, find the smuttiest thing around, get to her address, and pray that I don't catch a virus. But, St. Patrick's Day is different. During every St. Paddy's Day tons of kids swarm the local pub for the sole reason of getting wrecked. Seeing this flood of green idiots in my own hometown bar is painful. I imagine it's the same feeling athletes get when they see me in their gym the day after New Year's, dressed in new running shoes and a sweatband: they know I have no clue what I'm doing and odds are I'll be sweating heavily and puking in the bathroom in less than an hour. This is why you need to avoid your normal stomping grounds on St. Patrick's Day. Besides, there is a good chance you might tell a cop to "do something about it," or get in a fistfight over whether Grimus was a boy or girl. It's best to do that kind of stuff off of home turf.

Do Drink Guinness

The best part of St. Paddy's Day is delicious Guinness. (And, yes, it's Paddy not Patty. Patty is the lady in HR with the firemen calendar and all the cats.) Guinness is the holiest of Irish beers, probably because it most closely resembles a priest: it's got a black body, white collar, and one time as a child, I hung out with like nine of them and now I can't remember a thing that happened. Go figure! But any way you look at it; Guinness is a good idea on St. Paddy's Day. It's also lower in alcohol than most other beers—which will buy you a few more hours of fun in the bar before you wake up behind the abandoned Blockbuster covered in Taco Bell wrappers and missing your spleen.

Don't Yell, "CAR BOMBS!"

The Irish car bomb is the only drink used to celebrate a culture that is named after one of the darkest parts of that culture's history. Celebrating Irish heritage with a car bomb is like celebrating Black history month with a Jim Crow Cosmo. You can't name an ethnic drink after a tragedy in that country! That's like having a Japanese drink called the Nuke or celebrating America with an Alabama Slammer. It's just not right. So don't yell it out every two minutes at the bar.

Don't Drink Vodka

The only excuse for having a vodka cocktail in your hand on St. Paddy's Day is if you're throwing a Molotov at some riot police with a belly full of whiskey. Besides, top shelf vodkas are essentially $2.00 worth of alcohol in a $28.00 bottle. So, if you're going to walk into the house hammered, covered in piss, and screaming about "the Jews" again on this St. Paddy's day, at least do it with some class and smell like Scotch. I'm looking at you, Mom!

_Do_ Have Bottled Water by Your Bed

Believe me; you are going to wake up tired, confused, and wrapped in a blanket like a displaced Sandy victim. Your mouth is going to taste like you've been eating dirty bouncy balls and your clothes are going to smell like an old retainer case. Your first few moments of consciousness will be a flood of shame as you realize what you did the night before. Don't beat yourself up too much, it was St. Paddy's Day...and also everyone knows it's not gay if you pretended to be asleep when it happened. So, you're good. Just don't think about it. Grab the water, and start the recovery process.

Easy A-Moral

As I get older I find myself spending more time pondering the seemingly unanswerable questions in life. The questions the great philosophers have pondered since the inception of man: What is the meaning of love? What is it like to die? If Ann Coulter is on Fox, who's guarding Azkaban? Are Jody Foster's children considered foster kids? When Farrah Fawcett's kids breastfed, were they drinking straight from the Fawcett?

One question that I have been recently thinking about is, "Am I a good person?" I like to think I am. I like to think I'll go to heaven when I die but then again, I'm unsure what the benchmark is. Sure, I'm not a murderer but I'm no Mother Theresa either. I guess it comes down to whether or not God grades on a curve.

This concept creates another crisis of morality. If God does grade on a curve, then technically us "middle of the road" people should hate people like Gandhi and Mother Theresa. They would essentially be the nerdy kid in class who crushes every test and messes up the curve for everyone else. They would be making it harder for us to go to heaven. Furthermore, we should then be happy when we hear about awful murders and kidnappings. The murderers and rapists of this world would be that kid in class with a bad mullet who bombs the tests and turn everyone's C- into a B+. Do you remember that kid? I think his name was Ricky. What kind of world would it be if people hated nice people and loved horrible people?

When I think about this, I get nervous. There is plenty of evidence to support me being an awful person. Case in point: In 2011, a massive tsunami slammed into Japan's eastern coast killing thousands. News report, after news report flashed headlines like "Killer Tsunami" and "Japanese Tsunami." While this tragic event did make me feel sad, I also felt something else: hunger. Repeatedly seeing the word tsunami started a vicious craving for tiramisu. Specifically, the Japanese tiramisu at the local sushi place. After some emotional tug of war, I ordered a large tiramisu and ate it while watching the news. While this can hardly be considered a mortal sin, there is something inherently just wrong about it. Most of my moral shortcomings are on autopilot. They're never really premeditated. I've never been purposely hurtful, but I can be accidentally selfish. If I'm stuck in traffic and I see an ambulance with its lights on speeding down the shoulder, my first thought is not: "Oh, those people are going to go save a life." My first thought is: "no one is in that ambulance, those jerks just don't want to sit in traffic!" And even worse, if I sit in traffic for a long time I find myself thinking, "There better be cars on fire and bodies strewn about the street up there, or I'm going to be pissed."

During my second semester in college, I began to teach myself Gaelic. My Grandmother is *very* Irish and the only one in my family who knew the language. I thought this could be a great special connection that just the two of us could share. Sweet, right? Just wait. Shortly after I began studying Gaelic, my Grandmother got very sick. Her prognosis was grim. Obviously, I was very sad but also I began thinking that the ROI (another business term) of learning Gaelic had just dropped massively. She would call and ask, "How is the Gaelic coming, Ryan?" I would respond, "Um, well, how are you feeling, Grandma?"

When you send this kind of stuff out into the universe, it has a tendency to come back. It's called karma and it's real. Like, I know this guy who once grabbed his stepdad's nicotine patch and put it on over his eye, and then ran around the Christmas party yelling, "Look, I'm Glen, the Smelly Voice Pirate!" This was pretty funny at the time, but it turned out the nicotine in the patch absorbed into his eye and he had to spend the night sleeping at the doctor's office. It really hurt a lot, and I had to wear an actual eye patch for two weeks. I mean he...*he* had to wear a patch for two weeks. Anyway, the point is karma exists, and I probably have already dug myself a pretty deep hole.

Disappointment

I was waiting to board a flight, trying to figure out whom I'd hook up with if a *Lost* situation were to occur when I realized that there's a lot to be disappointed in these days. Heck, the fact that you spent money on this book may be coming to mind (but block it out). Think about baseball or that time you cried in front of the whole class cause you crammed a strawberry éclair in your Valentine's card box, and you didn't realize it would melt, and when it did, Ms. Duffy was like, "What's the matter with you?" and everyone laughed and laughed and Sara Dallar called you stupid, even though SHE'S the one who's stupid and you totally don't think of her when you are alone at night. Anyway, it seems silly to look for new things to be disappointed in, but I'm a privileged white person, and that's just part of my culture, so here we go. (It takes more muscles to frown than it does to smile...so consider this my workout.)

The first thing I'm upset about is adult twins. I'm really disappointed in the lack of adult twins who solve mysteries together. When you're young, twins are awesome. They dress alike and are usually solving crimes that their stupid parents are too oblivious to notice. But adult twins are disgusting. I instantly feel sick if I see adult twins next to each other unless they are on some stupid home design reality show.

I'm also really disappointed in lasers. I want you to sit down, take a deep breath, and really think about this: in two thousand and fifteen years of technology we solely use lasers in dance clubs for fun and for FIXING people's eyes! Not blasting holes through alien invaders, not slicing the tops off of mountains, but fixing some idiot's eyes in a relatively safe procedure that's over in a few minutes.

Next up on my list is kids. So disappointing! Kids nowadays are doomed—spending all day lazily on their phones and iPads. What kind of future minds are we creating? These kids are just staring at these devices—you know, the ones with the constant access to new ideas, different cultural perspectives, art, and international news. It's like, umm, put the phone down and go hang out with some trees, guys. It's called nature, ever heard of it? Go get a stick and hit some old tires in the woods like we had to do when we were your age. Ya know, "the woods," that place where murderers leave bodies and homeless people shoot heroin?! That's where you should be hanging out, not some AOL chat room on the FourSquare cloud! When I was a kid we didn't have WiFi and smart phones; we grew up with no exposure to people outside of our race, class, or culture. We got poison ivy on our buttholes and became isolated white-kid assholes who understood nothing about the world we lived in. It's called being a person, you lazy, idiot kids.

Graph #2

Breakdown of Trenchcoat Buyers

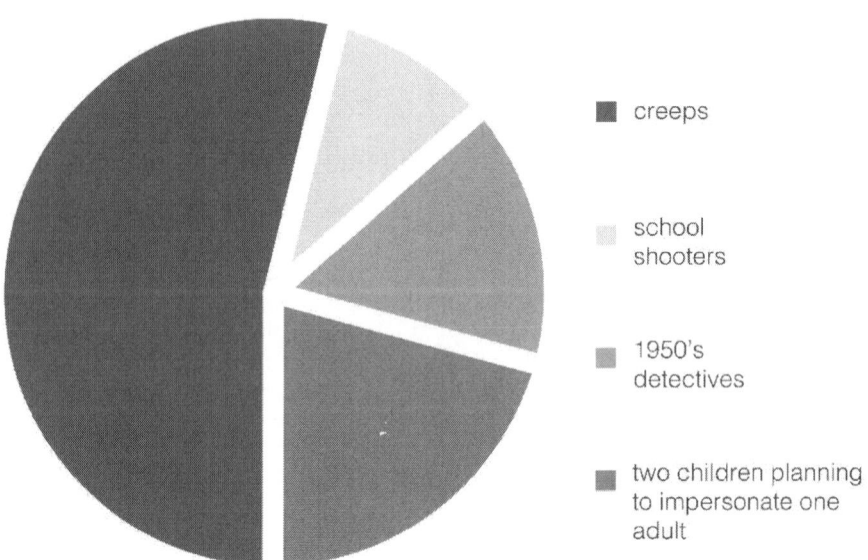

■ creeps

■ school
shooters

■ 1950's
detectives

■ two children planning
to impersonate one
adult

Excerpts from Diary #8

June 2, 2012

Dear Diary,

My friends say I have a Meth problem, but honestly, I think I have a "flying robots sent by the government to kill me are outside" problem.

June 13, 2012

Dear Diary,

I thought having an animated sign spinner guy to advertise the family business was a good idea, but Patricks' Funeral Home is still not doing so well.

June 14, 2012

Dear Diary,

I went to church today. My favorite part of church is when we get to judge all the parents with annoying crying babies right after the priest does the speech about being nice to people.

June 15, 2012

Dear Diary,

I just got home from the mall. The scary looking teens that hang out in front of Hot Topic called me fat Jimmy Neutron as I was leaving the food court.

June 20, 2012

Dear Diary,

Just finished modeling for an art class. It made me feel great. I know I look good naked cause the artists keep giving me the thumbs up every minute or so.

...And More Reflections

Tough Times

America has fallen upon hard times. Trust me, it's like all over the news. No one has any money anymore. I'm pretty sure the invisible hand of the market punched me in the nuts then took my wallet. I've tried to earn some money doing odd jobs here and there, but I was just eking by with that strategy. So I got a full-time job and now I'm just eking by in a tie and dress shirt.

My plan is to save up a little, then I'm going to open up a store of stupid-looking hats right next to Jason Mraz's house. I figure I'll be able to retire after a month or two and move to a mansion in the Hamptons. If that doesn't work, I want to design a motorcycle that is completely operated from the sidecar, just to drive it around screaming and freaking everyone out. That probably wouldn't make me a ton of money, but it would be hilarious.

Fighting to make ends meet is not easy. Sometimes I just hang out in banks hoping robbers take me hostage and I get a free pizza lunch. That rarely works, and I usually end up just huffing an empty Kiwi Strawberry Snapple for dinner.

Like I said, times are tough.

Successful people always say that the key to making good money is finding the one thing you are better at doing than everyone else, and do that. But I don't know what that is. I mean I'm really good at tangling iPod ear buds—like really fucking 'em up good. I'm also a good multitasker. For example, I usually cry and make love all at the same time. And people have also told me on numerous occasions that I am the Michael Jardan of typos. Unfortunately, I feel these are not very marketable skills.

Until I find my true calling, I will continue my daily 9 to 5 grind in the office. I'm not a big fan of working in an office. It's all the same "We made it to Friday" and "I need coffee" and "Someone pooped in the conference room!" jokes. (That last one is mine. Classic!) When I took the job, my plan was to sleep my way to the top but it turns out that actually involves sex and has almost nothing to do with napping under your desk like I originally thought.

Solutions

Friday nights are not just for smashing up Fritos and a bunch of old Nilla Wafers, spreading them all over my apt floor, strapping some roller-skates on my hands and feet, then pretending I'm a human Roomba and sucking them all up. It's also the night I come up with solutions for today's most pressing problems:

How to End Poverty

First up is the stigma of the homeless and impoverished in America. The homeless are persecuted in America, and it's a big problem. Heck, I'm guilty of it too. One time I saw a homeless couple making out and yelled, "Get a room!" Then I realized just how insensitive that was. My plan to solve poverty is very simple: it all comes down to spin. No, not the Persian nightclub where they found that hooker dead in a doggy carry-on bag. I'm talking about image, and almost no one has a worse image than poor people. So, instead of calling them, "The Poor," I propose we call them the "Super Eco-friendly." This small change could mean a world of difference. Instead of the local hobo, Rufus being a disgusting old alcoholic, collecting trash and pooping in the park, Rufus would be the super eco-friendly community member who uses no electricity, water, or gas. He composts his own feces in the park. He survives day-to-day solely on ethanol and collects recycling cans in a shopping cart regularly. He would be super green, and I'm not just talking about the multiple infected open wounds he has.

How to End Crime

Sometimes I take the train back and forth from work in Philadelphia. In Philly, we have "The Guardian Angels," which is a group of tough guy volunteers who patrol trains and help avoid crime and wear red hats. Philly's train system is pretty safe, and I often feel sorry for these volunteers who probably feel like they do not make much of a difference. Feeling like you're making a difference is important for job satisfaction and ultimately the safety of Philadelphia subway riders. That's why if I walk onto a car and I see a Guardian Angel, I lock eyes with him for a second and then look really mad and say, just audible enough, "Fuck!" Then I sit down and drink my Ecto Cooler juice box while staring menacingly at the other passengers and muttering, "You guys are so lucky...you have no idea."

How to Succeed in Business

My CEO invited me to his house this weekend. I figure it's going be a whole *Eyes Wide Shut* thing with people having weird sex, so I went ahead and bought a creepy bird mask. I wasn't sure if he was going to supply them or not and forgetting your orgy bird mask is probably a massive faux pas in the fancy business world, so I took the initiative to be prepared. Anyhoo, this got me thinking about business etiquette. (FYI: I've been to a lot of fancy work parties, and I consider myself to be a bit of an expert on high class aristocratic decorum at this point.) The important thing to remember is that it's all about the little things, the seemingly innocuous tiny details in these social interactions make all the difference. First off, be sure to say "bon-ah" not "boner" in conversation. For example: "There goes the Strategic VP of Interactive Services.... She gives me quite the bonah." That totally works, especially if you take a sip of champagne right afterwards. Believe me, they will all be really shocked and surprised at how refined and elegant you are.

How to Cure Alcoholism

Listen, quitting drinking is not that hard. I've done it like 9 times, but other people seem to really struggle with it, so I figured I'd present my solution. Many of my friends do this thing where they will take a sharpie and draw penises all over a friend's face if he passes out with his shoes on during a night of hard drinking. The ultimate goal, besides being hilarious, is to embarrass the victim so much that he handles his liquor a little better the next night he's out on the town.

This strategy, while common, is far from optimal. For starters, it often causes fights and resentment amongst hung-over friends in the morning. Thus I have developed an alternative technique that bypasses these unfavorable side effects. Instead of drawing penises on his face, I draw faces...on his penis. This is a WAY more effective strategy. Your friend will go home completely unaware of his new "scarlet letter." Then, while stepping into the shower, he will most likely look down and say something to the effect of, "What the fuck??? Someone drew Bart Simpson on my dick!" Trust me, it will be traumatizing. They will certainly never ask you or your other dipsomaniac friends about it. And he will always wonder—in the dark sticky places of his mind—if he was molested by Matt Groening or something horribly strange like that. Believe me, he will never pass out again and most likely cut back on his drinking habits.

How to Avoid Jail Time

Prison is a scary place. Personally, I don't think I would do well in prison...I'm just not a big fan of bunk beds. Also, cafeteria food? NO, THANK YOU! So I thought long and hard on how to not go to jail. The first tip I can offer is to be a white male and preferably rich and famous. Those people never go to jail. Seriously, it's ridiculous. For the rest of us, getting away with crime means being smart. Let's look at murder. If you're going to kill someone, wait till 1:00 a.m. on the first day of Daylight Savings Time. You see, on Daylight Savings Time the clock will go to 1:59 a.m. and then reset to 1:00 a.m. It's as if nothing happened during that hour—it's like that time I watched *Keeping Up with the Kardashians* or went to couples counseling. The idea here is how can you be held accountable for crimes you committed in a time that doesn't exist? It's foolproof! So what you do is, murder the person around the first 1:30 a.m., then once you're done, rush home and buy something online during the second 1:30 a.m. Then in court, you can be all like, "How could I be killing my wife at 1:30, if I was buying these LA Gear sneakers on eBay, your Honor?" It's a pretty smart move, and as someone who is reading a book written by a guy that the local Dollar Tree manager once called, "competent," you know all about smart moves by now.

State Your Name

I wonder if Kansas thinks Arkansas is kind of lame for making everyone pronounce its name as Arkan-saw instead of Arkan-sas? I imagine Kansas is kicking it with some friends at a party and someone (probably West Virginia, you know how he is) brings up Arkansas, and Kansas is like, "Oh, God, don't even get me started on her. Can you imagine if I started going around asking you guys to call me Kan-saw?! Haha! Hey guys, I have a fancy new name now. Please call me by my new name! It's ridiculous! I knew that bitch in high school, when she was just a bowlegged slut named Arkan-sas. Then she decided to class it up and tell everyone she's French in 1881, like, out of nowhere. Arkan-saw...pretending to be all fancy.

I wonder if she remembers that everyone Arkan-saw her blow Mike Bell at Jessica Martenelli's party junior year in the coatroom. Real fancy! She isn't fooling anyone. Hey Florida put that down. You're going to break it!! Florida, stop it. What is the matter with you? That's it! Who invited Florida? He has to leave now! I told you not to bring him!"

Cultural Differences

In 2002, I went to college at Villanova University—a private school outside of Philadelphia. Villanova allowed me the rare opportunity to meet and learn from a diverse group of students ranging from white, affluent kids from New Jersey to white, affluent kids from Connecticut. If you put all my friends in a row, it could easily look like the line at a Brooks Brothers store. I want to be clear, this doesn't mean that I'm not attuned to the pain of racial profiling, stereotyping, and prejudice. In fact, one time while working my job as a graduate research assistant during my Masters work, a professor assumed I was tech-savvy just because I was wearing a cashmere sweater and using a MacBook Pro! It's like, excuse me? That's called stereotyping. So minorities...I know your pain. We are one in our struggle. As you can probably tell, I consider myself a bit of a crusader for social justice. I won't even play with a Rubik's Cube because I think it teaches children to segregate by color, which is wrong.

Growing up in America usually means you're going to experience some cultural clashes. I think having contact with people who are different is important. Media outlets have become so siloed in specific ideologies and advertising has become so targeted that the same communities are having the same products, messages, and ideas recycled back to them. This creates a dynamic where one point of view is regurgitated to the same community over and over again, further solidifying it as the "right" point of view every day. So, since I'm liberal, I watch MSN where my own liberal ideas are fed back to me as news. Google knows I contribute to campaigns on education, so my banner ads stress a need for education funding. Every day I'm convinced further that my perspective on the world is the universal perspective. (This is why purposely being exposed to ideas outside of your world-lens is important.) Every encounter with a new culture is an opportunity to grow as a person and understand that you're not the center of the world. Just the other day, I went to the bathroom in an Ikea and their toilet was Swedish and different—not wrong, just different. It looked more like a vacuum than a toilet. I figured it out as best as I could. It was a real learning opportunity for me. Did you know the Swedish word for bathroom is "janitor closet"? Pretty cool! I was asked to leave for some reason. But my point remains the same.

We are often taught that there is only one way to see the world but there are lots. For example, my best friend is from New York. He calls large meaty and cheesy sandwiches on a long roll, "heroes." In Philadelphia, we call them "hoagies." If you went to a deli in my neighborhood and asked for an "Italian Hero," they would point to a picture of Rocky Balboa. (Note: All South Philly delis are legally required to have a framed photo of Rocky Balboa displayed at all times.)

Since I started living with my girlfriend, who is from California, I've noticed that a large cultural gap can exist even between two, middle class, pale, Irish, white kids. For example: If you order Chinese Lo Mein, in San Francisco, you will get what the East Coast calls, "Chow Mein," and vice versa if you're on the West Coast. This dynamic does allow for one distinct advantage: anytime I'm caught doing something dumb or strange, I can say, "You don't do that? It must be an East Coast thing." "It must be an east coast thing" has gotten me out of many situations. Accidentally put deodorant on over my dress shirt? It's an East Coast thing. Throwing batteries at cyclists during rush hour? It's an East Coast thing. Cocaine with breakfast? It's an East Coast thing. It's the perfect excuse. It's like that popular Shaggy song, "It Wasn't Me," but without all the sexism.

Excerpts from Diary #9

June 23, 2013

Dear Diary,

I was watching TV with my little nephews today. I doubt those Power Rangers would be doing flips and karate kicks and stuff. I did morphine once, and I could barely move. I just napped and called my dog "soft" all day.

August 19, 2013

Dear Diary,

You'd think people from South Carolina would have better teeth based on all the effort they put into keeping everything white and straight.

August 20, 2013

Dear Diary,

Big news! My girlfriend and I have decided we are going to tie the knot...in her fallopian tubes because we don't want anything to do with kids or commitment.

August 21, 2013

Dear Diary,

I realized something today: whenever I hear that little voice in my ear tell me that I'll never be good enough...I know I'm talking to my mom on Bluetooth.

August 22, 2013

Dear Diary,

I spent the day babysitting for my aunt and uncle. My annoying little cousin was bragging about how he sleeps in a racecar bed. Whatever, you little idiot.... I sleep in a real car.

Phases

An Outfit to Die For

I have been watching a lot of ghost hunter shows on TV recently. I think they're fascinating. If ghosts do exist, I never understood why they're always hanging out at little girls' sleepover parties and playing with Ouija boards. If I were invisible, I'd be in strip clubs or movie theaters all day long. Thus, I figure most of the ghosts that humans do encounter are all weird creepy pedophiles and all the cool chilled-out ghosts are just catching a Bond movie or rocking out at a Rolling Stones concert. So, most ghosts probably get a bad rap.

Sometimes I worry that when I die I will have to wear the outfit I died in for all of eternity in Heaven. The Bible never really covers this, but all the popular ghost shows I watch depict spirits wearing the outfit they died in. Civil War soldiers are still wearing their uniforms. The prom king who died in a drunk car accident is still wearing his letter jacket. This is why I will never scuba dive. For one, I get all pruney in water and secondly, can you imagine having to walk around in Heaven with a big old oxygen tank and stupid flippers for eternity? It would be a nightmare! Just try to imagine getting in an argument in Heaven and having the angels take you seriously in that ensemble. NO THANK YOU! I will also never try autoerotic asphyxiation. That guy has no friends in Heaven at all. Those guys probably have their own table in the cafeteria and everyone else gives them dirty looks. I know it's Heaven, and people there are all nice but when Jesus isn't looking those guys must get excluded from all the best cloud parties. You can't really lie about dying in a boating accident when you're standing there in Heaven with a belt around your neck and your pants around your ankles.

If I ever commit suicide, I'm doing it in my favorite casual outfit (sweat pants/Umbro windbreaker/Heelies), and I'm going to stuff my pockets full of Starbursts (no yellows). That way I'd be the coolest dude in all of Heaven.

"Move over, Steve Irwin; there's a new sheriff in town! Now, who wants some Starbursts?"

Palindrama

Dona: Hey, Ryan.

Me: Aloha, hola.

Dona: Thanks for inviting me to lunch. I always wanted to come here.

Me: Tis a top spot. A, sit.

Dona: Ok. Did I tell you that Dad got all mad at me for not going to Church with him?

Me: Wow.

Me: He did, eh?

Dona: Yeah, but I talked my way out of it.

Me: Pa's a sap.

Dona: Yeah. Mom was cool about it though.

Me: Ma is as tits as I am!

Dona: Yeah, she is pretty cool. Did they ever acknowledge that you sometimes try to talk only in palindromes?

Me: Dona, never even a nod.

Dona: Wait a minute, are you talking in palindromes now?

Me: ...Racecar?

Dona: This is why no one likes you.

Graph #3

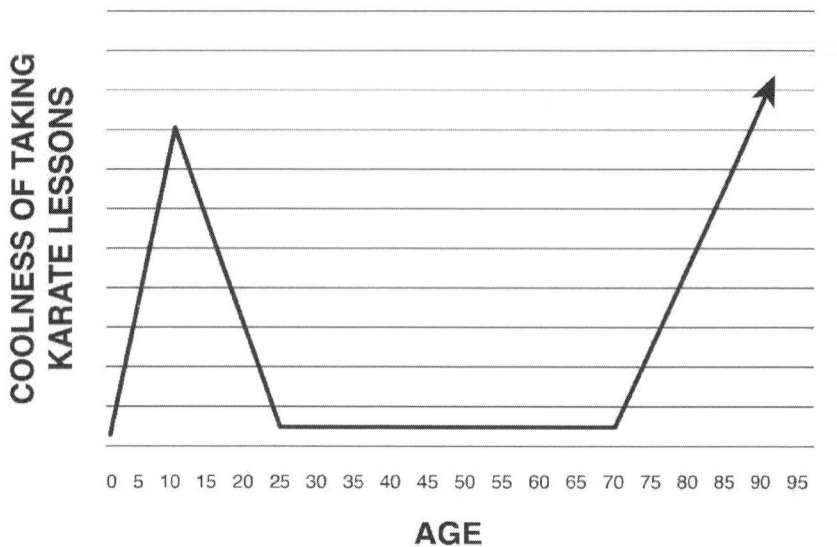

Going Through a Phrase

I'm a big fan of adages, quotes, and expressions. I think they're such a neat part of someone's personality. We all build our own little lexicon of sayings that we've picked up from family members, friends, ex-lovers, and the other characters that make up our life's novel. A little turn of phrase can instantly bring someone back to a time and place that may have been long forgotten. Here are some phrases and quotes I've been thinking about:

A New York Minute

A New York minute is just like a regular minute except after you pick it up from the train station, it spends the whole night talking about how great the city he lives in is and subtly hints that your city's pizza is subpar. It'll mention how annoying tourists are and how minutes in your city "go so slow." Odds are the New York Minute wasn't even born in New York, he probably just moved there like two years ago from Scranton to become an actor and to "show them!"

Children

Pablo Picasso famously said, "All children are artists. The problem is how to remain an artist once they grows up." I think a more accurate quote would be, "All children are artists. The problem is...none of them are any good. I can't even tell what that is. Trees are NOT red."

Pink Sky

"If you see a pink sky at night, sailor's delight. If you see a pink sky in the morning, you probably have a real job. Shut up and go to work, I'm trying to sleep here!"

A Baker's Dozen

I feel like the guy who coined the term "A baker's dozen" was really just a dumb baker who didn't know how much a dozen was.

I imagine him at the town market in his white baker's apron saying, "Excuse me sir, but there are only twelve roses here, and your sign clearly says they come by the dozen."

The florist then replies, "Umm, yeah, a dozen means twelve of something," in front of everyone.

Then the embarrassed baker is like, "Ooh, umm, well I'm a baker and for bakers a dozen means…umm thirteen. Yeah. That's it. Baker's dozens are different from your dozens. So, yeah, that's why I was confused. Yup. Okay, I have to go now."

Goody Two-shoes

This phrase always makes me laugh because it sounds like we resent someone for wearing two shoes. Like, *"Ooh, look at Sally with her TWO shoes, la di da. Is your limo here yet, your majesty? I'm Sally; I need to wear TWO shoes. I'm too good to just hop around like everyone else. I'm scared to get in trouble cause I don't want to risk my lavish second shoe! Haha! What a goody two-shoes!"*

What kind of Dickensian trash heap were these people living in that having two shoes meant you were prissy or no fun? If following the rules was the deciding factor between one or two shoes, then I might be okay with being a little overly moral. Also, how far could the mischievous kids get while running away with just one shoe on? If you really want to do some damage, you guys might want to consider wearing that second shoe, it's a pretty basic investment.

Ben Franklin

"It is better for people to think you are an idiot than to take your pants off in the supermarket and remove all doubt."

A Collection of Letters I've Written

Dear People Who Say "My Cat Thinks He's a Dog:"

No, he doesn't. Honestly, he has no idea about anything, even simple math or basic *Mighty Ducks* Trivia. Don't try and make your cat seem interesting, he is not. He is also not "kissing" you in the morning; he's licking the dried Sun Chip crumbs off your sweaty gross face.

Sincerely,

Ryan

Dear Turkey Hill Ice Cream:

I bought a tub of Red Raspberry ice cream as a treat, and to celebrate my weekly Jenga tournament win. The other players at the old folks home are awful—a coked-up Michael J. Fox would put up more of a fight. Anyway, after some much-deserved gloating, I picked up my ice cream, and I noticed it felt lighter and smaller than usual....

I called your customer service line to complain and was told the tub was not smaller; I had just gotten bigger, which was a smart ploy as I have been hitting Curves pretty hard these days. But then I noticed that instead of saying half gallon it said 1.5 quarts.

One and a half quarts? Really, Turkey Hill? You're lucky I don't know the Metric system, and refuse to learn it—cause I'm a patriot—but I'm keeping my eye on you.

These colors do NOT Run! USA, USA!

Sincerely,

Ryan

Dear Ludens Cough Drops:

I congratulate you on having the bravado to break into the cough medicine market with nothing but pure candy. The balls it must have taken to look at all of your competitors—testing spices and natural remedies on focus groups—and then to calmly say, "Fuck all that, just re-package those Jolly Ranchers and put them in the cold and flu aisle. Trust me. It'll work."

You are a true testament to American vigor, courage and laziness. You're like my real dad: I only see you once or twice a year, I know you don't work...and against my better judgment, I will always choose you.

Sincerely,

Ryan

Dear God:

I just have one question for you: "Jared Leto"...how did you let that happen? I just can't fathom it. Were you just like, "Oh, I know, we just made this Ryan guy with a lazy eye and an irrational fear of both vaginas and road signs, now let's make this

Jared guy and let's make him the most handsome guy on Earth. And you know what, let's make him a really talented actor, too. Oh, and he could probably use some musical talent. Yeah, let's give him the voice of an angel. Oh, and let's throw in a chiseled body that defies all laws of gravity and time."

I mean, WTF! How is any guy supposed to attract any girl with Jared Leto out there in the world?! I'm just saying, my stories from Space Camp and my CK1 magazine cologne are not going to cut it with this guy around. Most of the time I'm just a grown man singing Another Bad Creation's "Iesha" and complaining about yellow Skittles. All I'm saying is you could have diversified your stock in mankind a little better, God. Spread the wealth around, Man.

Jared Leto is amazing. I heard when his mom was pregnant with him she could all of a sudden do back flips—like big ass gator back flips standing flat on the ground. Then, the second he was born—boom! She couldn't do them anymore. That sets the bar pretty high. So thanks for the help there, God. Way to throw an outlier (Malcolm Gladwell reference) down here and fuck up the curve for everyone else. Real dick move, Man.

Sincerely,

Ryan

Dear Catholic Church:

I'm not sure why you have such an issue with women using birth control. Sure, having a poor, single, thirteen-year-old girl become unexpectedly pregnant worked out for you once, but by your own account that was a freaking miracle.

Yours in Christ,

Ryan

Excerpts from Diary #10

January 19, 2014

Dear Diary,

Went to lunch with the grandparents today and realized I make the same noise when I see a guy in jeans & sandals as my grandpa does when he sees interracial couples at Arby's.

February 3, 2014

Dear Diary,

Tried to pepper-spray a mugger with my inhaler this morning. We both got a good laugh out of it. Mondays…. Am I right??

February 24, 2014

Dear Diary,

I made an important realization today. I read all my emails in either Tom Hanks's or Meg Ryan's voice.

March 5, 2014

Dear Diary,

My cousin wanted to play Marco Polo at the pool today, so I dressed him up like a 13th century merchant explorer and put him on a boat to Asia. Weird kid.

March 16, 2014

Dear Diary,

I really want to get into teaching youth ice hockey...so I've been working on getting a DUI.

April 7, 2014

Dear Diary,

I accidentally brought this orphan into a mom & pop shop today. It was awkward.

Thoughts While Stepping out of a Moving Vehicle

Time Machine

People love talking about what they would do if they had a time machine. There've been moments where I wish I could've turned back the clocks too. One time at a fancy restaurant I ordered the catfish, and thirty minutes later the waiter brought me this weird, chubby, emo chick who looked nothing like her online profile pic! It was awkward. Don't worry, that's not what this article is about. This piece is about how I'm a little bit fed up with people automatically assuming that time machines are also teleportation machines. Everyone who's had this awful conversation always says, "Oh, if I had a time machine, I'd kill Hitler!" Well, unless you live in Vienna—no, you wouldn't. You can't get on a plane with nail clippers these days; there's no way you're bringing your time machine. And you couldn't travel back in time and then hop on a plane to Germany cause you don't exist. Think about it. You wouldn't have a license or passport or anything. Your money wouldn't even be real.

So really, if you had a time machine, you would be pretty much stuck going back in time to see your own boring town every day. You would probably be confined to like a mile radius of your house. You would probably just find out that your dad sold weed in high school and your mom had an abortion when she was fifteen. It would be awful. So if you're a scientist spending your time working on time travel, just stop. Focus on inventing more important scientific breakthroughs like dinner pills, hoverboards or a way for men to comfortably eat ice cream cones in public.

Questions

1. Does the artist Seal like Shark Week?
2. Were there less prima donnas, pre-Madonna?
3. Are accomplished dentists ever awarded with some kind of dental plaque?
4. I wonder what do they say to the guy who designs drawing boards when his ideas fail? "Back to...umm...your desk, idiot."

5. Is Olive Garden's slogan, "When you are here, you are family," is designed to welcome customers, or to discourage them from having sex in the bathrooms?

6. Do they have continental breakfast in Hawaii?

7. Are "corn mazes" repetitive for Native Americans?

8. How do you say, "I have spazzy hands" in sign language?

9. Can I set my sleep number mattress to 90 proof?

10. If you strip at both gay and straight strip clubs, does that make you bi-poler?

11. Why does the WWE leave folding chairs all around the wrestling ring? People keep cheating, guys. It's not rocket science!

12. How can my new raincoat be "Dry Clean" only?

13. Are all bumper stickers based on Jimmy Buffet songs or are all Jimmy Buffet songs based on bumper stickers?

Dolphins

Everyone is always going on and on about how cute and great dolphins are, and I have to be honest, I'm pretty sick of it. I don't understand why the public can't see dolphins for what they currently and historically are—a bunch of bottle-nosed disease-torpedoes. That's right, you heard me. They are always goofing off; bouncing around beach balls like it's a goddamn Dave Matthews Band concert. "Oh, sweet, he's definitely gonna play two-step, bro!" *No, he's not, you gross hippie dolphin! Get a real job.* Don't even get me started on the dolphin's constant need for attention.

"I'm going to do a bunch of flips like an F'in show off and totally steal all the attention away from Ryan's devil stick performance during the family cruise." It's like, we get it...you can do a flip. Congratulations! You know, there's a lot more to parkour than just a single flip, guys. Frankly, I'm not impressed. People always say one-trick ponies, but it should be one-trick dolphins if you ask me.

Dolphins are always squealing and laughing like schoolgirls too—always smiling with their decrepit Kristen Dunst razor jigsaw teeth. *What's so funny, dolphins? Are you laughing at me because you ruined my devil stick performance and embarrassed me in front of everyone? That's fine. We'll see who's laughing when I'm on* America's Got Talent *and Howie straight loves my devil sticking.* You're just going to be floating around the ocean playing sonar and running that back flip game of yours straight into the ground.

Everyone acts like dolphins are SOOO smart too. Well, I for one have never seen a dolphin do anything "highly intelligent." Not swimming into a big tuna net or not getting your face stuck in 6-pack soda rings seem like pretty simple concepts to master. Yet, our brilliant dolphins can't seem to figure it out. *Look, he got stuck in sea garbage again? What a genius! We should give him the Nobel Prize for smartness! Oh, did I say Nobel? I meant DUMBBELL!*

Dolphins are idiots. They probably only seem smart because they hang around Florida. Anyone standing next to Florida seems smart by comparison. I will tell you one thing: dolphins are definitely not smart enough to learn the subtle skills needed to be good at devil sticks. SUBTLE: that is a word you won't find in a dolphin's vocabulary.

I for one am glad the Navy uses dolphins to find underwater mines designed to blow up submarines. Nothing would make me happier than to see some attention-hoarding dolphin doing flips, ruining the d-stick routine I spent all night practicing, and then diving real deep, and...all of a sudden—a satisfying muffled boom, and a bloody dorsal fin floats to the surface a few seconds later. Music to my ears! *Not laughing now, are you dolphin?!*

Okay, everyone! Gather 'round. This trick is called the helicopter!

Never Buy an Apartment from the Barenaked Ladies

It's 2:00 a.m. in my apartment formally owned by the Barenaked Ladies and I just caught the lead singer coming through my window:

Me: Jesus Christ, you scared the hell out of me. What are you doing here?!

BNL: This is my old apartment...this is where I used to live.

Me: Yeah, I know. What are you doing here? You can't just break in.

BNL: Is that new paint. Why did you paint the walls?

Me: Umm...cause I LIVE HERE! Are you serious right now? You can't break into my house and then act like I'm the dick for painting my own walls.

BNL: Don't tell me you cleaned the floor too! Jesus!

Me: Listen man, I'm gonna call the cops if you don't leave right now.

BNL: Hold on—is that my dish rack and mouse trap? Why did you keep the dish rack?

Me: I dunno. You left it here when I bought the apartment from you like a year ago, and I needed one.

BNL: These things used to be mine. ...I guess they still are.

Me: No, no they are definitely not. But if you want that dish rack and the disgusting mousetrap, you can take them, just get the fuck out! I got work in the morning.

BNL: This would make a good song.

Me: What did you do to my phone?!

Excerpts from Diary #11

April 23, 2013

Dear Diary,

Everyone is making such a big deal about that Life of Pi movie. So you had a tiger in your boat? Big effing deal. I had a wasp in my Prius yesterday.... Where's my award?

May 4, 2013

Dear Diary,

The lady at the supermarket asked if I knew how to check myself out...I told her I've done it at four different rehabs this year, I'm sure I can figure it out. Then I booked it out the door to a liquor store.

May 15, 2013

Dear Diary,

Today I heard a guy say, "If you think raising one kid is hard, try having three!" ...which I thought was horrible advice.

May 26, 2013

Dear Diary,

Finally went to go see a soccer game. None of these guys are doing back-flips, so foosball is basically bullshit.

Acknowledgments

Writing this book was a true labor of love. If you would have told me I'd be the author of a book when I was just a young boy playing in the streets of Philadelphia, I would've probably yelled, "Stranger danger!" and peed myself while running away. I was really afraid of being kidnapped and stuff when I was younger.

Anyway, I'd like to thank my girlfriend, Chelsea, for letting me grow a beard and develop a serious drinking problem—from what I understand, are both prerequisites for writing a decent book. Thank you to all the wonderful friends who've helped. I have a tremendous group of creative friends who have graciously offered their time and talents to make this a reality. They also put up with me when I talked about this project incessantly, and insisted they introduce me as a "published author" to people at parties. A special thanks to Chelsea Moylan, Jill Bruschera, and Haley Nahman for their amazing graphic design work, creative input, and support. I also wanted to take this time to address the publishing house rumors that were going around. It's true that I had originally secured a deal with a major publisher, but there were some issues. They called me on the phone to ask the title of the book, and I told them to call it, *Broken: Ryan Patricks*. Unfortunately, they printed 30,000 copies entitled, *Broken Colon Ryan Patricks*. I refused to allow them to be released, so now it's a whole legal thing, and I decided to go with a smaller publishing company, which is the way cooler thing to do anyway.

I want to thank the great pieces of literature that have always inspired me: Joyce's *Ulysses*, Hemingway's *Farewell to Arms,* and of course, Tolstoy's *War and Peace*[4]. These classics have always been there for me like old friends. Whenever I found the wells of inspiration dry, I could count on these friends to replenish my creative pint.

I'm also especially grateful to my editor, Lisa. A lot of people said I wouldn't be able to write a book. Outside of lacking any formal education or basic reading/writing skills, I cannot type. My hunt and peck typing method made this project extremely time-consuming. Fun Fact: I actually started writing this book when I was twelve years old. This forced my editor to cut large chapters from the book that were outdated including: "Why am

---

[4] Actual inspirations: *Highlights Magazine, Zoo Books: Giraffes and the Drink-ology* recipe book.

I getting hair...down there?" "Gym Class Boner," and "Ryan Patricks: Dunkaroos Enthusiast." (Technically, I wrote that last one just a month ago, so we probably could have kept it.) While I consider myself a writer, I have the grammar and spelling capabilities of a dyslexic foreigner. Sometimes my chapters looked as if I typed them wearing mittens. My Spellcheck could officially file unfair labor practices against me at this point. Paying attention to grammar and spelling is important. For example, there is a world of difference between "a trophy wife" and "atrophy wife." That mistake cost me $10,000. I paid for a mail order bride and essentially got an oversized doorstop, but that's a story for another day. So, thank you, Lisa, for your hard work. You have made this book almost readable...and I know that wasn't easy.

Lastly, thank you, whoever you are, for buying this book. Of all the things you could have bought, you bought this, and I appreciate that. You may have bought it because you're a good friend, or perhaps you wanted to support amateur comedy writing. Maybe you bought this book because you thought it would be funny (if so, I'm so sorry). Maybe, just maybe, you bought this book because you still owe me ten bucks from when we went to the movies together and I paid for the cab and you were like, "Oh, I'll get the popcorn." ...But did you get the popcorn, Carl? You, in fact, did no such thing. Perhaps you thought I had forgotten about that popcorn years ago, and you are reading this now and just realizing that I did NOT, in fact, forget about the time you basically robbed me blind. Whatever your reason was for buying this book, I thank you! You are super nice and dare I say, much more physically attractive than the average person.

You have officially made it to the end of the book and you should be proud of yourself, unless, of course, you just skipped to the end of the book as soon as you got it. If that's the case, here is a spoiler alert: the little kid's therapist is actually an oblivious ghost the whole time! Okay, now start from the beginning; it will all make so much more sense.